A CROC IS NOT A GATOR

An animal guide

To Carter,
Enjoy!

By F. Elza Cooperman

Illustrations by Aleksandar Andjelkovic

www.is-not-books.com

info@differenttrails.com

© 2018 by Different Trails
ISBN-13: 978-1-7322098-0-0

Photography and design: F. Elza Cooperman
Copy editing and proofreading: Scott Weikert

Thanks to:
Raymond Larabie for Still Time font
Vecteezy for free vector art

Different Trails

WHY DO DIFFERENCES MATTER?

I suppose if you are on safari and something very large with lots of sharp teeth suddenly lunges at you from the water's edge, you're probably not going to care whether it's a crocodile or an alligator… you're simply going to run. But once you're safely back in camp and your heartbeat has returned to normal, then the question might be of more interest.

Differences can tell us a lot about the evolutionary history of an animal as well as how its environment helped shape it. Animals can look similar for different reasons.

1) They stem from a common ancestor. This is known as *divergent evolution*, where one species *diverges* (or splits off) into multiple descendant species. A good example of this is wolves and domesticated dogs.

2) *Convergent evolution* is when two organisms are not closely related but end up having similar features. This is often the result of environmental factors which push them to *converge* on (or move toward) a specific form. Sharks (which are fish) and dolphins (which are mammals) look a lot alike because their streamlined body shape is the most practical for swimming quickly through the ocean.

Let's take a quick look at how evolution has shaped camels. They didn't always have humps and live in the deserts of Africa and Asia. They started off about 50 million years ago in the woodlands of North America and were the size of a rabbit, with long legs and no hump.

Many millions of years later, the climate started to cool and the tropical forests began to recede. Camels had to change to survive. They grew bigger; their necks became longer, and their feet flattened out. They then began traveling in all directions, slowly adapting in size and shape to fit into their new environments. Those that traveled into South America some three million years ago became modern day llamas and alpacas.

Others went west and crossed the land bridge into Asia, where they needed to adapt to a more arctic and desolate terrain. They became larger still, grew a thick coat, and their feet became even flatter and wider. They also developed a double hump to survive long periods of scarce food and water. These were the Bactrian camels.

But some continued on, down into Africa, where it was much hotter and drier. Their double hump merged into a single one and their hair became shorter. Welcome the arrival of the dromedary!

Unfortunately for the camels still in North America, the climate continued to change too quickly and they all became extinct about 10,000 years ago, along with mammoths and sabertooth cats. But the legacy of that first, tiny camel lives on in the rest of the world.

DEFINITIONS

GEOGRAPHY

NEW WORLD - North, Central and South America and the surrounding areas
OLD WORLD - Africa, the Middle East, Asia, Australia and the surrounding areas
NORTHERN HEMISPHERE - the half of the Earth north of the Equator
SOUTHERN HEMISPHERE - the half of the Earth south of the Equator

In the late 1400s, European explorers found the American continents. Previously, it was believed that the world consisted only of Africa, Asia and Europe. This extremely different "fourth part of the world" became known as the Western hemisphere and the New World, to differentiate from the now Eastern hemisphere and Old World. These terms are now used to conveniently distinguish animal locations and origins.

LIFESTYLES

HERBIVORE - an animal that eats only plants
CARNIVORE - an animal that eats only meat
OMNIVORE - an animal that eats both plants and meat
SCAVENGER - an animal that eats dead plants and/or animals
INSECTIVORE - a plant or animal that eats insects
DETRIVORE (or detritivore) - an animal that eats decomposing plants and animals
EXUDATIVORE - an animal that eats tree gum, sap or resin

DIURNAL - active during the day
NOCTURNAL - active at night
CREPUSCULAR - active during twilight (dawn and dusk)

Animals are active at night for a variety of reasons: to avoid the heat of the day in hot climates, to use the cover of darkness as protection (when prey) or camouflage (when a predator), or to lessen competition. Since mountain lions hunt during the day, coyotes can easily share the same territory by hunting at night.

DEFENSES

TOXINS are molecules that can affect the nervous system, the immune system or even dissolve flesh.

VENOMOUS animals bite or sting to inject their toxins. Think of snakes, spiders, lizards, bees, ants, wasps, jellyfish and even the platypus.

POISONOUS animals unload their toxins through contact (absorption through the skin), ingestion or inhalation. Examples are frogs, toads, and salamanders.

The lionfish is venomous but not poisonous (it can be safely consumed), while the garter snake is not venomous but poisonous (its body absorbs and stores the toxins of its prey, such as newts and salamanders). Some salamanders are both venomous and poisonous.

TAXONOMY

Taxonomy is the scientific method for naming organisms. It's constantly changing as new information is discovered but it gives scientists a clear way to talk about a specific animal without getting muddled down in disagreements about common or popular names. Each animal has a unique name (in Latin) and is grouped with other similar animals, which in turn are part of a larger group. For example, the common house cat is:

Kingdom:	Animalia (all animals)
Phylum:	Chordata (those with a hollow dorsal nerve cord)
Subphylum:	Vertebrata (those with a backbone)
Class:	Mammalia (mammals)
Order:	Carnivora (meat-eaters)
Family:	Felidae (all cats)
Genus:	*Felis* (small and medium cats)
Species:	*catus* (domestic cat)

There are six prominent groups of animals:

INVERTEBRATES lack a backbone and comprise over 95% of all animals. They include worms, sponges, cnidarians (coral, jellyfish, anemones), echinoderms (starfish, sea urchins), mollusks (gastropods such as slugs and snails; bivalves which include clams and oysters; and cephalopods such as squids and octopuses) and arthropods. This last group includes arachnids (horseshoe crabs, spiders, mites, scorpions), myriapods (millipedes, centipedes), crustaceans (lobsters, crabs, shrimp, barnacles) and over 800,000 species of insects (butterflies, beetles, ants, flies, ladybugs, mosquitos, grasshoppers, termites, cockroaches, dragonflies, fleas).

FISHES have backbones, live in water and have gills, scales and fins. There are over 25,700 species. They include bony fish (tuna, salmon), cartilaginous fish (sharks, rays) and jawless fish (lampreys). Seahorses are fish too!

REPTILES are born on land, cold-blooded and have scaly skin. There are over 8,100 species. This includes crocodilians (crocodiles, alligators), tuataras, scaled reptiles (lizards such as chameleons, iguanas, geckos, monitor lizards and legless lizards; and snakes which include boas, pythons, cobras, sea snakes and vipers) and turtles (tortoises, terrapins).

AMPHIBIANS are born in water with gills but develop lungs when they grow up. There are over 5,400 species. They include frogs, toads, salamanders and newts.

BIRDS hatch out of hard-shelled eggs and have feathers. There are over 9,700 species. They include hawks, penguins, kiwis, hummingbirds, ostriches, chickens, water birds, pigeons, flamingos, sea gulls, storks, cranes, vultures, owls, parrots and many more.

MAMMALS drink milk as a baby and have hair. There are over 4,700 species. Some main groups are:

- Echidnas, platypuses
- Marsupials (opossums, bandicoots, koalas, wombats, possums, sugar gliders, kangaroos)
- Placentals
  - Tenrecs, aardvarks
  - Hyraxes, elephants, manatees
  - Sloths, anteaters, armadillos
  - Primates (lemurs, monkeys, apes, humans)
  - Lagomorphs (pikas, rabbits, hares) and rodents (squirrels, beavers, gophers, guinea pigs, rats, mice, voles, hamsters, capybaras, chinchillas, porcupines, gerbils, prairie dogs, marmots)
  - Hedgehogs
  - Moles, shrews
  - Even-toed hooved animals (camels and llamas; swine such as pigs and peccaries; hippos; ruminants including deer, pronghorn, giraffe, cows, goats, sheep and antelope) and cetaceans (whales, dolphins)
  - Odd-toed hooved animals (horses, zebras, tapirs, rhinos), bats, pangolins and carnivores (cat-like including cats, hyenas, aardwolves, mongooses and civets; and dog-like such as dogs, bears, skunks, weasels, badgers, otters, raccoons, walruses, sea lions and seals)

It's interesting to note that whales and dolphins are in the same group as deer and camels. Evidence shows that 50 million years ago they were the same animal… a raccoon-sized, omnivorous, land animal. Then slowly, over millions of years, whales returned to the sea.

Legs turned into fins; they adapted from fresh to salt water; and their buoyancy reduced so they could stay underwater. They held their breaths longer (up to an hour and a half); they became more efficient at using the oxygen that entered their lungs (90% as opposed to 15% for humans); and their nostrils conveniently moved to the top of their heads (the blowhole, which expels warm *air* from their lungs. It only looks like water due to immediate condensation in the colder outside air). Their pelvises became smaller and separated from the backbone, allowing them to move their tails up and down, rather than back and forth like fish do. The undulating body motion of a whale swimming is very similar to that of a dog running.

Despite their aquatic lifestyle, they still retain features from their terrestrial ancestors. They breathe air, nurse their young, and have similar skeletal features. For example, the bones inside their front fins resemble small arms and hands, and buried deep inside their bodies are still the tiny remnants of hindlimbs.

A similar story holds true with walruses and seals sharing a common terrestrial ancestor with bears and weasels.

CROCODILES

- Crocodiles have a long snout that **NARROWS** at the tip.
- In crocodiles, the upper and lower teeth line up, but since crocodilians don't have lips, the teeth remain **VISIBLE** even when their jaws are closed. This gives the crocodile its famous smile. The two, longer fourth teeth in the lower jaw fit into notches on the outside of the snout and point upwards almost like tusks.
- Crocodiles are **VERY AGGRESSIVE** and can be quite dangerous. Nile crocodiles attack and kill 300 people in Africa every year. Some Indo-Pacific crocodiles are even more deadly.
- There are 13 species of crocodiles. They are found throughout the tropical areas of **AFRICA**, southeast **ASIA**, **AUSTRALIA** and even Central America. The American crocodile lives throughout the Caribbean. The Nile crocodile from Africa is what we think of when we think *crocodile*.

CROCODILIANS all split off from a common ancestor about 75 million years ago. They're divided into three main groups:

- Crocodiles
- Alligators, caimans
- Gharials

NICEST SMILE?

ALLIGATORS

- Alligators have a short, wide, **ROUNDED** snout that is often very flat and smooth.
- Alligators have **HIDDEN** teeth. The lower teeth fit inside the upper row, and the long, fourth tooth is hidden in a special hollow pit in the upper jaw. In very old animals, these teeth can grow so long that they actually pierce the upper jaw and stick out the top.
- While still very dangerous, alligators are **LESS AGGRESSIVE** and don't move as well as crocodiles on land. Some zookeepers are even willing to walk across the backs of alligators while cleaning their pools. They would never try this with crocodiles!
- There are only two species of alligators. The American alligator lives in the southeastern **UNITED STATES** (mostly Florida). The Chinese alligator is found in a small part of eastern Asia. Alligators are not as sensitive to cold.

The **GHARIAL** or gavial is a slender crocodilian with a long, narrow snout. There's only one species that lives in the rivers of northern India. **CAIMANS** live in South America. They are quicker, more agile, and more crocodile-like in their movements.

LEOPARDS

- Leopards are found in **AFRICA** and **ASIA**.
- Both leopards and jaguars have spots, which are actually rings called *rosettes*. Leopard rosettes are much **SMALLER** and have **NO SPOTS** inside them.
- Leopards have an **EVEN** pattern all over their bodies.
- Leopards are **SMALLER**. They have a **SLIM** flexible body and triangular head. A fully grown male leopard weighs about 120 pounds.
- Leopards have **LONG** powerful tails, which help them leap into trees and balance on branches.
- Leopards live in a variety of habitats including jungles, mountains, grasslands and deserts. They climb **TREES** and will even carry their kill (up to three times their own weight) high into the branches to protect it from scavengers such as hyenas and lions.

There are 37 **SPECIES** of wild cats. These animals are different enough from each other that they could never have cubs together in the wild even though they may look similar (leopards, jaguars, cheetahs) or share the same name (snow leopards, clouded leopards). Sometimes in zoos, different species can have cubs, but these cubs can't have cubs of their own. A lion/tiger cub is called a *liger* and a jaguar/leopard cub is called a *jagulep*.

THE DIFFERENCE?

JAGUARS

- Jaguars live in the tropical rainforests of **CENTRAL** and **SOUTH AMERICA**.
- Jaguars have **LARGE** rosettes with one or more **SPOTS** inside.
- Jaguars have an **UNEVEN** pattern, with larger rosettes on the back, smaller ones on the neck and shoulders, and large solid black spots on the legs.
- Jaguars are much **LARGER**, weighing up to 300 pounds. They have a **STOCKY** body and round head.
- Jaguars have **SHORTER** tails since they spend most of their time hunting on the forest floor.
- Jaguars love the **WATER** and are seldom far from a river or lake. They're good swimmers and are known to go fishing by waving their tails over the water in order to attract hungry fish.

Technically there is no such animal as a **BLACK PANTHER**. Panther comes from *Panthera* (the big cat group of lions and tigers). Long ago, people thought there was a specific species of black cat called a panther, but today we know they are just darker versions of leopards, jaguars and even mountain lions. It's more accurate to say a black leopard or black jaguar. These animals do have spots but they're just very difficult to see on a background of dark fur.

BIRDS OF

HAWKS

- Hawks are in the same family as eagles, kites, buzzards, goshawks, harriers and Old World vultures. This description is based on *accipiters* (forest or true hawks such as the Cooper's hawk). The illustration is of a **RED-TAILED HAWK** (a *buteo* or soaring hawk).
- Hawks are small to **MEDIUM**-sized birds. They have **SHORT**, broad, rounded wings with a long narrow tail.
- Hawks are very fast but can still make tight turns and weave through **TREES**. When hunting, a hawk waits on a branch with good visibility. If it sees a small bird or squirrel, it **HIDES** while circling closer until flying down in a sudden burst of speed. The hawk gives up the chase if the prey isn't caught quickly.
- Hawks mostly flap and then **GLIDE** for a while.
- Hawks usually build simple **NESTS** out of twigs, weeds and roots, which they then line with moss or other soft green plants.

The definitions are often inconsistent, but basically a **BIRD OF PREY** eats meat (small birds and mammals) from hunting or carrion. A **RAPTOR** is a predatory bird with a hooked beak, keen eyesight and catches its prey with its strong talons (claws). A vulture is a scavenging bird of prey but not a raptor. Birds that eat fish and insects are not considered birds of prey, but the osprey is a fish-catching raptor. Some raptor definitions exclude night-hunters such as owls. Classification isn't always easy!

A FEATHER?

FALCONS

- Falcons are in the same family as kestrels, merlins (pigeon hawks), hobbies and caracaras. This description and illustration are of a **PEREGRINE FALCON** (the fastest bird in the world).
- Falcons are **SMALLER** and slimmer, with **LONG** tapered wings that are pointed at the tip.
- Falcons are extremely fast and like wide **OPEN** spaces with straight line views. Falcons hunt by circling high overhead and **SWOOPING** down at speeds of up to 150 miles per hour. They use fast, strong flight to pursue their prey. A falcon has round nostrils with an inner bony protrusion that prevents air from rushing into its head too rapidly when it dives (so it can still breathe at such high speeds). People have copied this design when building jet engines.
- Falcon beat their wings **STEADILY** and usually do not soar.
- Most falcons scrape out a small **HOLE** in the ground instead of building a nest.

These birds have extremely good **EYESIGHT**, up to eight times better than humans. Some hawks can spot a grasshopper 300 feet away. Hence sayings such as *eagle eyes* or *eyes like a hawk*.

BATS

- Bats are generally **SMALLER**, with large ears and a tail. They're found all over the world except in very cold areas. The smallest bat weighs only one-third of a penny.
- Bats mostly eat **INSECTS**. A bat can catch 600 mosquitoes per hour and eat up to 3,000 insects per night. Some bats also eat fish, frogs, lizards, birds or even small rodents.
- Bats use **ECHO LOCATION** (or *sonar*). They emit high-pitched squeaks through their noses or mouths as they fly. These sounds bounce off objects and echo back to their ears. Bats basically *hear* their food. Most calls are beyond our range of hearing.
- Most bats live in dark **CAVES** in enormous colonies, which can contain up to several million individuals. Some also live in small groups in hollow trees and around houses. Each bat has its own special place on the wall and is extremely loyal to the cave where it was born.
- **VAMPIRE BATS** do not suck blood. Instead they lick up blood after painlessly making a small cut on a sleeping animal with their razor sharp teeth. They feed on all kinds of mammals such as horses, cattle and sometimes even humans. There is little blood lost and the victim is seldom harmed.

A bat's **WINGS** are basically very long fingers covered with a thin, hairless piece of skin. This is very different from a bird, whose wings are fixed. A bat can scoop things up with its wing, cradle a new baby or wrap a wing around itself like a shawl. Wing shapes differ too, with swift fliers having long, narrow wings and slow fliers having broad, rounded ones.

DRIVE ONE BATTY!

FRUIT BATS

- Fruit bats are **LARGER**, with small ears and no tail. They live in tropical areas of the Old World, can weigh up to two pounds and have a wingspan of five feet.
- Fruit bats feed mostly on **FRUIT**, nectar and pollen. Many trees have special, large white flowers with a dank odor that attracts them. Some fruits (such as bananas, peaches, mangoes, avocados and cashews) depend on fruit bats for pollination or seed dispersal.
- Fruit bats find their food by **SIGHT**. They have large eyes that give them good night vision. They are further assisted by an excellent sense of smell.
- Fruit bats often hang upside down on the branches of tall **TREES** in large groups called *camps*.
- **FLYING FOXES**, the largest of all bats, are named for their fox-like faces and reddish-brown fur. They don't land very well and will often simply crash into a tree… and other flying foxes, which usually upsets everyone involved.

After rodents, bats are the most numerous mammals on earth. The **DIFFERENCE** between bats and fruit bats is so great that many biologists believe they must have had different ancestors, with the smaller bats descending from insectivores (shrews) and the larger bats descending from primates (monkeys).

DEER

- Deer have **ANTLERS**. Antlers are branched and made of solid bone. They're only on males (except for caribou) although some females have small stubs. Antlers **DROP OFF** after the fall mating season but grow back each year with an additional branch. Antler growth depends on diet and is not neccessarily an indication of age. They begin as spongy tissue covered by a furry skin called *velvet*, which is shed once the antlers are fully grown and hard.
- Deer use their antlers to **IMPRESS** females and scare off competing males during the mating season.
- Deer are found in **NORTH AMERICA**, **EUROPE** and **ASIA**. Africa only has one species.
- Deer are fairly **UNIFORM** in appearance, although size ranges drastically from the ten-pound pudu to the 950-pound moose.
- Most deer are **FOREST**-dwellers but can range from tundra to tropical rainforests.
- Deer are **SLOWER**. White-tailed deer can run 35 miles per hour (mph) but can only maintain that speed for short distances.

Deer and antelope are **EVEN-TOED** hoofed animals, which includes pigs, hippos, camels, llamas, giraffes, cattle, buffalo, sheep and goats. Antelope are actually more closely related to cows than deer.

THEIR POINT?

ANTELOPE

- Antelope have **HORNS**. Horns are unbranched, hollow and made of *keratin* (like fingernails). Both males and females have **PERMANENT** horns (although they're often smaller on females). Shapes vary greatly: straight, spiked, twisted, ridged, spiral, curved, lobed, long or short.
- Antelope horns are for **DEFENSE**, in fighting off predators or rivals within their own herd.
- Most antelope are native to **AFRICA**. Others live in Asia, India and the Middle East. There are no true antelope native to the Americas.
- Antelope are more **DIVERSE** in shape. They include wildebeest, kudus (pictured here) and gazelles. In general, antelope are smaller than deer.
- Most antelope live in open grasslands and **SAVANNA**, but they're also in woodland, desert, semi-aquatic and even cold environments.
- Antelope are **FAST**. A springbok can't quite outrun a cheetah (the fastest land animal at 75 mph), but it can give it a good workout at 55 mph. Unlike the cheetah that can only run in short bursts, the antelope can maintain a speed of over 25 mph for long distances.

The **PRONGHORN** of North America is not an antelope. Instead, it is in its own family with no close relatives. They have branched (pronged) horns that are shed annually. The horns attach to the skin instead of the underlying bone.

BUTTERFLIES

- Butterflies are active during the **DAY**. At night or during bad weather, they hide under leaves or crawl into rock crevices.
- Butterflies are often **BRIGHTLY** colored. This warns predators that they're poisonous or taste bad, although no butterfly is toxic enough to kill a large animal. Other butterflies copy these colors to pretend to be dangerous even though they're not. Colors help males and females recognize each other. Dark colors soak up warmth from the sun, allowing butterflies to fly in cool weather. Butterflies have different patterns on the upper and undersides of their wings. Their right and left sides are also not exactly the same.
- Butterflies are **SMOOTHER** and more slender.
- Butterflies have **CLUBBED** antennae that are long, thin and shaped like a golf club.
- Butterflies rest with their wings folded **UPRIGHT**, although they may open them when sunning.
- Butterflies make a shiny **CHRYSALIS** above ground when they undergo metamorphosis.

Because *butterfly* is such an old **WORD**, we don't really know where it comes from. Some think it's from *butter-colored fly*; others say it's from the yellow substance around newly emerged butterflies. People even once believed that butterflies stole milk and butter. In other languages, their name has nothing to do with either *butter* or *fly*.

DAY AND NIGHT!

MOTHS

- Most moths are active at **NIGHT**. They're attracted to light but no one really knows why. It could be due to an overload of their light detectors or maybe their flight is influenced by the heat (the wing nearest the light flaps slower, which causes the moth to turn towards it).
- Moths are usually **DULL** looking. These colors and patterns help them blend into the background for protection. Some day-flying moths copy the patterns of poisonous butterflies or even bees. Many have large, eye-like markings on their wings to scare predators.
- Moths are **HAIRIER** than butterflies.
- Moth antennae are short and **FEATHERY**. Since a male moth has to find his mate in the dark, these extra feathers increase the surface area to help him detect her scent.
- Moths rest with their wings open **FLAT**.
- Most moths build a silk **COCOON** underground when they change from their caterpillar stage. The cocoon of the domesticated silkworm moth is the source of commercial silk.

Some caterpillars turn into butterflies but most turn into moths.
Moth types outnumber butterfly types sixteen to one. In many ways, one can say that butterflies are just **FANCY MOTHS**.

RABBITS

- Rabbits are **SMALLER**, more compact, and have **SHORTER** ears and legs. They **RUN** instead of leap.
- Rabbits live in underground burrows and prefer areas with lots of **COVER**. When a predator is near, they hide, crouch low and remain perfectly still. If necessary, they'll scamper short distances in a zigzag pattern to escape.
- Rabbits are social and live in **GROUPS** called *colonies*.
- Rabbits are **BLIND, HAIRLESS** and helpless when they are born. They don't open their eyes for seven to ten days. The mother makes a soft **NEST** of grass and her own fur. A young rabbit is called a *bunny*, even though we often use this pet name for any rabbit.
- The **COTTONTAIL** is the most common wild rabbit in North America. Its name comes from its puffy tail, which serves as an alarm signal when raised. All **DOMESTIC** rabbits descend from the wild rabbits of Europe and Africa. They range from pure white to all black, from short fur to long silky fur, and from short ears to long floppy ones.

Rabbits have long been associated with spring and new life due their highly reproductive nature. They're first mentioned as an **EASTER** symbol in Germany in the 1500s. Children believed if they were good, the Easter bunny would lay a nest of colored eggs.

SPLITTING HAIRS?

HARES

- Hares are **LARGER** and have **LONGER** legs and feet. Their ears can have black tips and are longer than their heads. They make long, high **LEAPS** and can run up to 50 miles per hour.
- Hares like **OPEN** spaces. They usually try to escape enemies by running, and their large ears help them hear predators far away. To rest, they will crouch next to a clump of grass with their long ears flattened against their back.
- Hares live **ALONE**. They only meet in pairs for mating.
- When hares are born, their eyes are **OPEN** and they have a full coat of **FUR**. They're able to **HOP** almost immediately and don't need a nest. A young hare is a *leveret*.
- Desert **JACKRABBITS** are actually hares. Their name comes from their long, donkey or jackass-like ears. The small **SNOWSHOE HARE** looks like a rabbit except during winter when it's all white with black-tipped ears.

Rabbits and hares are not rodents. They belong to the group **LAGOMORPHA** (which also includes pikas). While the common names of rabbit and hare are often used interchangeably, their true classification differences are listed here.

TURTLES

- Turtles live in or near **WATER**. Most are in fresh water. All turtles, even those living in the ocean, breathe air and lay their eggs on land.
- Turtle shells are **FLATTER** and streamlined. This reduces water resistance while swimming. One species of turtle has a shell covered with moss so it looks just like a rock when it sits still.
- Turtles have long toes and **WEBBED** feet.
- Turtle are **HERBIVORES** or **CARNIVORES** but rarely both at the same time. Carnivorous turtles mostly eat fish.
- The **LEATHERBACK** is the largest turtle. It can be over seven feet long and weigh up to 1,200 pounds. Unlike other turtles, its head is too large to be pulled in. It lives in the ocean and eats jellyfish and plants. **TERRAPINS** are the only turtles that live exclusively in the brackish (salty) waters of marshes and river inlets along the coast.

Turtles are the **OLDEST** living reptile. They existed 200 million years ago with the early dinosaurs. These ancient turtles could not pull their necks in.

WIN THIS RACE?

TORTOISES

- Tortoises live strictly on **LAND**, mostly in hot, dry areas. They use water only to drink or bathe. They do not need to lay their eggs near water like turtles do.
- Tortoises have high, **DOMED** shells. All shells consist of an upper portion (*carapace*) and a lower portion (*plastron*) which are joined together at the sides.
- Tortoises have short toes and blunt, **CLUB**-shaped feet. Their limbs are covered with hard scales. Some burrowing tortoises have flattened front limbs and heavy nails. Because they can dig and hide underground, tortoises can live in temperatures over 140°F .
- Tortoises are strictly **HERBIVORES**, eating flowers, shrubs, grasses and cacti. The moisture in these plants is enough for adults to survive over a year without drinking. They may also dig holes and then wait by them when it looks like it might rain.
- The **GALAPAGOS TORTOISE** can be as long as four feet and weigh over 500 pounds. The Seychelles giant tortoise can live over 180 years.

The **WORDS** tend to be used differently around the world. In the USA, turtles are in water, tortoises on dry land and terrapins in brackish water. In the UK, turtles are in oceans, tortoises on land and terrapins in freshwater. In Australia, a tortoise is everything except sea turtles. In general, however, if the back legs are webbed, call it a turtle; if they're stumpy, call it a tortoise.

STOP MONKEYING

MONKEYS

- Monkeys are generally **SMALLER** and have **TAILS** (except for a few Old World monkeys).
- Monkeys are found in many areas around the world. They're **COMMON** in tropical areas of Africa, Asia and South America.
- Monkeys live in **TREES** and are excellent climbers, but a few live on the ground. Since they can't swing their arms like apes (only the spider monkey can), they move by **RUNNING** along the tree branches on all fours.
- Monkeys are **NOT AS SMART** as apes.
- Old World monkeys or *true monkeys* are more closely related to apes than other monkeys. They include **BABOONS** (and mandrills), **MACAQUES** (the rhesus monkey, shown here), langurs (leaf monkeys) and guenons. New World monkeys include **HOWLER MONKEYS** (whose loud calls carry for miles), capuchins, **SPIDER MONKEYS** and marmosets (including tamarins).

Apes and monkeys (and humans) are **PRIMATES**. The term *ape* was often used incorrectly for all tailless monkeys (such as the Barbary Ape which is actually a type of macaque). Now it's only used for Old World primates that are most closely related to humans. Everyone else is basically a monkey.

AROUND!

APES

- Apes are **LARGER** and **TAILESS**.
- Most apes are **ENDANGERED** and only live in a few areas in the Old World.
- Most apes live on the **GROUND**. They walk on all fours but some can walk short distances on two legs. They can **SWING** though the trees using brachiation (swinging arm-over-arm) like Tarzan.
- Apes are generally more **INTELLIGENT**. In the wild, they use various self-made tools. Trained chimpanzees can learn to communicate with humans by using sign language.
- There are basically two groups of apes. The *great apes* include **GORILLAS** (pictured here, the largest and most powerful), **ORANGUTANS** (which means *man of the forest* in Malay) and **CHIMPANZEES**. The small or *lesser apes* include **GIBBONS** (such as the black siamang).

As much as 98.8% of the genetic material (**DNA**) of chimpanzees is identical to humans. But if we're so much alike, how can we still be so different?

If each human cell contains three billion pieces of information, then 1.2% still equals 35 million differences. Some of these have a bigger impact than others. Also, even two identical pieces of DNA can work differently if they are turned on in different amounts, places or times.

THE ANSWER IS

BEAVERS

- Beavers are **LARGER**. They range from three to five feet long (with up to two feet of that being the tail). Weighing between 35 and 60 pounds, they're the world's second largest rodent.
- Beavers are **REDDISH** brown to black.
- Beavers have a **WIDE** tail that's flattened **HORIZONTALLY**, like a paddle. A beaver can slap its tail loudly on the water's surface as a warning signal for danger.
- While swimming, beavers and muskrats look very similar. Beavers, however, have **LARGER** ears that stick up. Typically, most of their body is under water, leaving only their large, wedge-shaped **HEADS** visible.
- Beavers have **FIVE** distinct toes on their front feet. Their hind feet are **WEBBED**.
- Beavers are **HERBIVORES**. They use their large, sharp teeth to acquire their favorite food… the soft underlayer of tree bark. They also eat roots and water plants.
- Beavers build large **STURDY** lodges made of logs (that they cut down themselves), large sticks and mud. They also build dams in order to create deeper ponds for their homes.
- Baby beavers stay with their parents for **TWO** or more years.

While both are **RODENTS**, muskrats are more closely related to hamsters than to beavers. They look similar because of convergent evolution (their aquatic environment shaped their appearance). While muskrats get their name because they resemble a rat, they are not closely related to true rats.

GNAWING AT YOU!

MUSKRATS

- Muskrats are **SMALLER**, reaching only two feet in length (half of that is tail). They reach a maximum weight of four pounds.
- Muskrats have a **GRAYISH** underfur covered with long dark or yellowish brown hairs.
- Muskrats have a long **SKINNY** tail that's flattened **VERTICALLY** (meaning it has flat sides). It uses its tail as a rudder to swim through the water.
- Muskrats have **SMALL** short ears that are sometimes hard to see. While swimming at the surface, usually their heads and whole **BODIES** are visible.
- Muskrats also have five toes on their front feet but only **FOUR** are clearly visible. Their hind feet are only **PARTIALLY** webbed.
- Muskrats are **OMNIVORES**, eating primarily grasses and water plants. If food is scarce in winter, they'll eat small animals such as crayfish, mussels, insects, fish and amphibians.
- Muskrats build smaller, **FRAGILE** lodges. Made of only cattails and marsh vegetation, these homes can wash away in spring floods. Muskrats sometimes move into beaver lodges. The beavers appreciate the extra set of eyes looking out for predators.
- Baby muskrats leave home after about **ONE** year.

Sometimes river otters (in the weasel family) and nutrias (closely related to guinea pigs and chinchillas) are **MISTAKEN** for beavers and muskrats, especially while in the water.

LIONS

- Lions belong to the big cat group of **PANTHERS**. This includes tigers, jaguars and leopards.
- Lions **ROAR** but can't purr. The ability to roar depends on the structure of the hyoid bone, to which the muscles of the trachea (windpipe) and larynx (voice box) are attached.
- Lions live in **AFRICA**, with one species in India. They used to be extremely widespread but now only live in fragmented populations.
- Lions roam open grasslands and **SAVANNAS**.
- Lions are **LARGER**, with the bigger males weighing up to 550 pounds.
- Lions are more **DIURNAL**, meaning they're active during the day.
- Lions are **SOCIAL** and live in prides. Pride size varies from three to 20 adults, depending on habitat and food availability. Females cooperate when hunting and can take down much larger prey such as zebra, buffalo and even giraffe.
- Males and females look **DIFFERENT**. Males are larger and have a prominent mane. The lion is the only cat with a tuft of fur on its tail.

The cat family is split into two main groups: modern cats (including lions and mountain lions) and **SABER-TOOTHED CATS**. These were found world-wide, existed for about 42 million years, then went extinct about 11,000 years ago. Their big canine teeth could be up to 11 inches long!

OF THE BAG!

MOUNTAIN LIONS

- Mountain lions belong to the small-and-medium-sized cat group of **FELINES**. This includes lynx, ocelots, servals, caracals, jaguarundis, cheetahs and house cats.
- Mountain lions **PURR** but can't roar. They can also make high-pitched chirps and whistles and low-pitched hisses and growls. They're famous for their loud screams.
- Mountain lions live throughout the **AMERICAS**. They have the greatest range of any terrestrial animal in the Western hemisphere.
- Mountain lions are extremely **ADAPTABLE**, living from sea level to snow-covered mountain peaks. They also dwell in swamps, coastal forests, woodlands and high deserts. They prefer areas with dense underbrush and cover.
- Mountain lions are **SMALLER**. Males typically weigh from 200 to 220 pounds.
- Mountain lions are both **NOCTURNAL** and **CREPUSCULAR**, hunting at night and twilight.
- Mountain lions are **SOLITARY**. They'll ambush their prey by suddenly leaping onto its back from a hidden position.
- Males and females look very **SIMILAR**, although males can be up to 40% larger.

A mountain lion, cougar, puma, catamount and Florida panther are all the same animal. Because this cat is so widely distributed, each region has their own **NAME** for it. In fact, it holds the Guinness record for the animal with the greatest number of names, with over 40 in English, 18 in South American languages and 25 in native North American ones.

CENTIPEDES

- Centipedes have **ONE** pair of legs on each body segment (which may number up to 200).
- Centipedes are **FAST** moving, flexible and somewhat flat. They have long antennae.
- Centipedes are **CARNIVORES**. They hunt insects and caterpillars.
- Centipedes are **VENOMOUS** and kill their prey by injecting it with venom contained in modified legs (called *maxillipeds*) on their first segment. Centipedes can bite people, which can be painful but usually isn't life threatening. As with a bee sting, it can cause an allergic reaction.
- Centipedes are **BRIGHTLY** colored to warn other animals of how dangerous they are.
- Amazonian centipedes can grow over a foot long and are very **AGGRESSIVE**. Giant centipedes in the forests of Madagascar have been known hunt mice and rats.

Both centipedes and millipedes are **ARTHROPODS** (a group including insects, crustaceans and spiders), but they are not very closely related.

STEP AHEAD!

MILLIPEDES

- Millipedes have **TWO** pairs of legs per body segment. They have fewer segments (up to 100).
- Millipedes are **SLOW**, somewhat rigid, slightly cylindrical in shape and have shorter antennae.
- Millipedes are **DETRIVORES**, with a diet of damp and decaying wood and plants. They help recycle rotting plant material.
- Millipedes are **HARMLESS**, although some have a noxious secretion used to deter predators. They don't bite and aren't venomous. When threatened, they coil into a tight ball.
- Millipedes are **BROWNISH**.
- The giant African millipede can grow 15 inches long and is kept as a **PET**. The shocking pink dragon millipede secretes a toxin that smells like almonds. Cave millipedes have adapted to their environments and are blind and ghostly pale.

Many people believe that centipedes have 100 **LEGS** (since *centi-* means 100), but they can have anywhere from 30 to 354 legs. Interestingly, there are no centipedes with exactly 100 legs. While *milli-* means one thousand, different types of millipedes have a different number of legs. The most legs any millipede has, however, is only 750.

CROWS

- Crows are **SMALLER**, about the size of a pigeon. They're generally black but they can also have some white, gray or brown coloring.
- Crows have a **FLATTER** bill and a **SQUARE** tail. Their feathers are rounded at the tip and lay flat on their chests.
- Crow wings are more **BLUNT** with a splayed wing tip. Their wingbeat is usually **SILENT**.
- Crows are **MORE** adaptable, able to live just as easily in big cities as in nature.
- Crows are omnivores (eating anything edible as well as many things that aren't!) but prefer **VEGETABLE** matter and crops (especially corn). Farmers will use scarecrows to protect their fields, but since crows are extremely smart, the straw figures quickly become perches rather than deterrents.
- A crow call is a higher-pitched **CAW**. They can make at least two dozen different sounds.

Crows and ravens are basically **IDENTICAL** in color, shape and behavior. Many people use the terms interchangeably, but technically, ravens can be called crows but not all crows are ravens.

CROW ABOUT!

RAVENS

- Ravens are one-third **LARGER** than crows, with a larger wing span and four times the weight. They are black with a blue-purple gleam to their feathers.
- Ravens have a larger, heavier, **CURVED** bill and a **WEDGE**-shaped tail. Their feathers are slightly pointed, giving their chests the appearance of a small mane (or *ruff*) when puffed up.
- Ravens have **POINTED** wings that sometimes make a loud swishing **SOUND** during flight.
- Ravens are **LESS** adaptable in terms of their habitat, preferring wild, open areas.
- Ravens are also omnivores but rely more on **CARRION** (especially sheep). They are very cautious and may wait to approach a potential food site until several crows are present.
- Ravens have a low and slow **CROAK**. They can express themselves with hundreds of different vocalizations.

A **GROUP** of crows is called a *murder* based on the belief that they would gather together to judge the bad behavior of a flock member. If found guilty, that bird would be killed. This story probably comes from the fact that crows will feed on their own dead. Because they also scavenge human remains, both crows and ravens are associated in European cultures with death, cemeteries, battlefields and execution sites. As such, a group of ravens is called an *unkindness* or a *conspiracy*.

AFRICAN ELEPHANTS

- African elephants are found in sub-Saharan **AFRICA**.
- African elephants are significantly **LARGER**, with the males being 13 feet at the **SHOULDER** (their tallest point) and weighing over 15,000 pounds.
- African elephants have **BIGGER** ears that cover their shoulders. Ears radiate heat, so a hotter climate requires larger ears. They have a **SINGLE** dome on their heads, and their skin is looser and more wrinkled.
- Both males and females have large **TUSKS** (modified incisor teeth). These are used for defense and to dig for food. The tip is the oldest part.
- The trunk of the African elephant has **TWO** fingers at the tip.
- The savanna elephant has **FOUR** toes on its front feet and **THREE** on its back feet. The forest elephant, however, has five front toes and four back toes.
- African elephants aren't easily domesticated and are **HUNTED** by poachers for their ivory tusks.

The word *elephant* comes from the Latin *ele* (arch) and *phant* (huge). The three species (two African and one Asian) are the largest living land animals. Elephants don't **DESCEND** from mammoths or mastodons. Mastodons split off from a common ancestor some 30 million years ago, while mammoths and elephants branched off from each other around 5 million years ago.

FORGET THIS!

ASIAN ELEPHANTS

- Asian elephants live in southeast **ASIA**, ranging from India and Nepal to Indonesia.
- Asian elephants are **SMALLER**, with the largest males reaching only nine feet at the top of their **BACK** arch (their tallest point) and weighing up to 13,000 pounds.
- Asian elephants have **SMALLER** ears, a **TWIN**-domed head and a long, tapered lower lip.
- Only some males have tusks. The rest (and some females) have small tusk-like teeth called **TUSHES**, which are barely visible and only seen when the mouth is open.
- An Asian elephant has **ONE** finger on its trunk tip. It compensates by holding objects against the underside of its trunk.
- Asian elephants have **FIVE** toes on their front feet and **FOUR** toes on their back feet.
- Asian elephants were **TAMED** some 8,000 years ago. They've been used for carrying heavy objects, war, ceremonies, hunting, traveling over rough terrain, and modern day safaris.

TRUNKS evolved because an elephant's head is so high from the ground. This way, they don't have to bend down to eat or drink, which would put them in a vulnerable position. This long nose is used for smelling, breathing, trumpeting, drinking and picking up items. It has over 40,000 muscles!

SQUIRRELS

- Squirrels are found almost **WORLDWIDE**. They live in the Americas, Europe, Asia and parts of Africa, and have even been introduced to Australia.
- Squirrels are **LARGER**. They generally range from 12 to 20 inches long (including the tail) and weigh from one to two **POUNDS**.
- Squirrels have large **BUSHY** tails, which are almost the same length as their bodies. When they run, they hold it **HORIZONTALLY**, straight out behind them.
- Squirrels are a **SOLID** color, usually black, gray, red or brown. They don't have any stripes.
- Squirrels can live **SIX** to eight years. Unfortunately, many of them are killed during their first year due to food shortages and inexperience with cars.
- Squirrels make their homes in **TREES**. They build multiple **NESTS** of leaves, twigs and bark either within tree branches or in hollows such as abandoned woodpecker holes.

The squirrel **FAMILY** includes tree squirrels (described here), ground squirrels, pygmy squirrels, giant squirrels, flying squirrels, chipmunks, marmots and prairie dogs.

THE OLD BLOCK!

CHIPMUNKS

- Chipmunks are mainly found in **NORTH AMERICA**. One species lives in northeast Asia.
- Chipmunks are **SMALLER**. They can be six to 12 inches in length and weigh a mere one to four **OUNCES**.
- Chipmunks have short, **THINNER** tails. When they run, they hold their tails **VERTICALLY**, straight up in the air.
- Chipmunks have distinct **STRIPES** running the entire length of their faces and bodies. They're usually tan in color with white and black stripes.
- Chipmunks typically live about **THREE** years. They can to live up to nine years in captivity.
- Chipmunks live **UNDERGROUND** in extensive **BURROWS** which can extend up to 30 feet long and have several tunnels and hidden entrances. Although they can climb trees like squirrels, they spend more time on the ground.

GROUND SQUIRRELS look very similar to chipmunks but are slightly larger (although not as big as tree squirrels). They have a stripe only on their bodies, not across their faces. Instead, they often have a white eye ring.

SEA URCHINS

- Sea urchins are *echinoderms* (Greek *ekhinos* meaning spine and *derma*, skin). This group includes sand dollars, **SEA STARS** (starfish), brittle stars, crinoids (sea lilies) and sea cucumbers. *Urchon* is an old English word for hedgehog.
- Sea urchins are **SMALL**, ranging from one to four inches across.
- Sea urchins look like a spherical **PINCUSHION**. They have a **HARD** internal skeleton (called a *test*) covered by a skin.
- Sea urchins have long, pointed **SPINES**. Some are thick and blunt; some are thin and sharp; some are over 12 inches long. A few are even venomous, capable of killing a human. Spines offer camouflage, protection and help with movement.
- Sea urchins are **MOBILE**. They're covered with hundreds of tiny, flexible, adhesive tube feet.
- Sea urchins have a **TUBE**-shaped digestive system, with various parts performing different functions. The mouth is located on the underside and they expel waste from the top.
- Sea urchins feed mainly on **ALGAE** but will also eat decomposing matter such as dead fish.

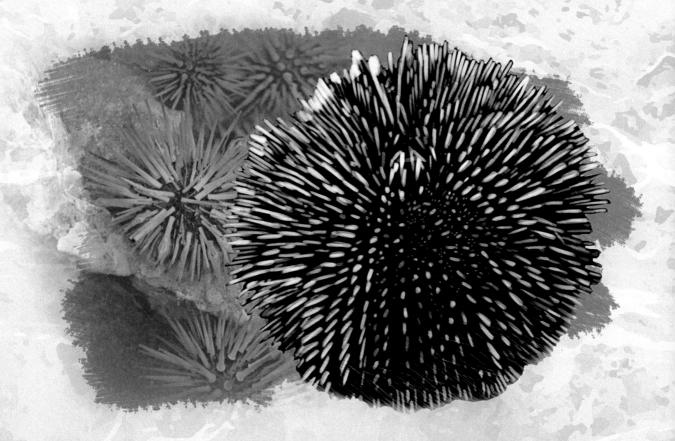

SAND DOLLARS are a flat type of sea urchin. What you find on the beach is actually the skeleton, without the velvet-like skin of spines. After it has been bleached white in the sun, it is said to resemble an old Spanish or American silver dollar coin.

SOMETHING TO SEA!

SEA ANEMONES

- Sea anemones are *cnidarians* or creatures with stinging cells (Greek *knide* meaning nettle). Their relatives are **JELLYFISH**, hydras and corals. They're named after the anemone flower because of their colorful appearances.
- Sea anemones **VARY** in size. Most are two inches or less wide, but some can get up to almost six feet across.
- Sea anemones look like a tubular **FLOWER**. They have **SOFT** bodies with no solid skeleton. They maintain their shape through their fluid-filled cavity, which acts as a hydrostatic skeleton.
- Sea anemones have a ring of **TENTACLES** on top. Covered with stinging capsules, these allow the anemone to paralyze small swimming animals. All anemones are venomous but only a few are dangerous to humans.
- Most sea anemones are **SEDENTARY**, anchored to a rock or the sea floor by an adhesive foot.
- Sea anemones have a **POUCH**-shaped or sac digestive system. One body cavity performs all the functions. Its mouth, located on top, also serves to expel waste.
- Sea anemones eat the **FISH** and marine invertebrates they catch with their tentacles.

How can **CLOWNFISH** live among anemones without becoming dinner? They're covered by a mucus layer that protects them from an anemone's sting. In this symbiotic relationship, the clownfish is safe from predators, and the anemone gets the leftovers from the clownfish's meals.

KANGAROOS

- Kangaroos are **LARGER**, with the males reaching heights of six feet and weights of 200 pounds. Females are about half the weight.
- Kangaroos have **LONG**, oversized hind legs that are designed for moving **QUICKLY** on flat, open terrain. Their knees and ankles are set far apart, making their legs seem out of proportion to their bodies.
- Kangaroos have **DULL**, muted colors evenly distributed over their bodies. Colors include blacks, grays and reddish browns. Some have white patches on their face, legs and ears.
- Kangaroos eat mostly **GRASS**, so their teeth show this. Their molars are tall and curved, with ridges designed for cutting. They lack premolars (between the front teeth and back molars).
- Kangaroos live **LONGER**, with a lifespan of 20 to 25 years. They grow more slowly and stay with their mothers longer.

Both kangaroos and wallabies are marsupials (they have a pouch to carry their babies) and belong to the **FAMILY** of macropods (meaning *large-footed*). There over 50 species in Australia and New Guinea, which also include wallaroos, tree-kangaroos, hare-wallabies, rock wallabies, pademelons, quokkas and potoroos.

IN THEIR STEP!

WALLABIES

- Wallabies are **SMALLER**. Their size can vary from one to three feet tall and from four to 50 pounds.
- Wallabies have **SHORT**, compact hind legs. This enables them to move with great **AGILITY** through dense forest areas.
- Wallabies have **BRIGHTER**, glossier coats. They usually have two to three different colors, which include black, gray, red, beige, brown or white. Some also have distinctive stripes on their cheeks and hips.
- Wallabies feed mostly on forest **LEAVES**. They have flat molars (for crushing and grinding), premolars, and also a special, sharp tooth for occasional cutting needs.
- Wallabies have **SHORTER** lives, between 11 and 15 years.

A **WALLAROO** is not the offspring of a kangaroo and a wallaby. Instead, it is its own species. It is physically more like a kangaroo (just slightly smaller and lighter) but its genetic make-up is closer to some wallabies. It also tends to be more sedentary and solitary in nature, unlike both kangaroos and wallabies who move around in groups called *mobs* or *troops*.

DOLPHINS

- There are over 30 species of **OCEANIC** dolphins, such as bottlenose and spinner dolphins. The five species of **FRESHWATER** dolphins are named after the rivers they live in (such as Amazon, Yangtze or Ganges). Their smaller eyes are an adaptation to muddy river water.
- Dolphins are **LARGER**. Sizes vary from five to 25 feet and weights range from 150 to 1,500 pounds. Orcas can reach a length of 30 feet and weigh up to eight tons.
- Dolphins have **SLENDER**, streamlined bodies. They have a taller *dorsal* (back) fin that is hooked or **CURVED** towards the tail.
- Dolphins have a distinct protruding snout with a **POINTED** beak. They have up to 100 sharp **CONE**-shaped teeth.
- Dolphins are more **TALKATIVE** and can make whistling sounds through their blowholes to communicate with each other underwater.

Dolphins and porpoises appear to have a permanent **SMILE**. The way their jaws line up causes the corners of their mouths to be permanently upturned. Actually, they can't really smile at all.

IT ON PORPOISE?

PORPOISES

- There are only six species of porpoise, including the Dall's porpoise. They live close to **SHORE** and are usually quite shy. As a result, they're less likely to ride alongside the bows of ships. The harbor porpoise is in danger of extinction in the Celtic Sea from being caught in fishing nets.
- Porpoises are **SMALLER**. They rarely grow longer than six feet and weigh under 300 pounds.
- Porpoises are **PLUMP** and stocky with rounded, torpedo-shaped bodies. They have a small, low, **TRIANGULAR** dorsal fin.
- Porpoises have **BLUNT** snouts without a beak. Their teeth are shaped like **SPADES** or shovels.
- Porpoises are **LESS VOCAL** and perhaps even lack the ability to make certain sounds due to structural differences in their blowholes.

All dolphins are **WHALES** but not all whales are dolphins. Whales are divided into two groups, which separated from a common ancestor some 34 million years ago. Baleen whales (such as humpback and blue whales) have *baleen* (filtering plates made of *keratin*) and two blowholes. Toothed whales have teeth and one blowhole. This group includes dolphins, porpoises, pilot whales, sperm whales, narwhals, belugas and orcas. For centuries, the word *whale* was used for any large animal in the sea. Even though they are now in different groups, the original names remain. Otherwise the killer whale might have to be renamed the killer dolphin… which doesn't sound nearly as scary!

WHAT'S

BEES

- Bees have a **FUZZY** appearance. They have baskets on their hind legs for carrying pollen.
- A worker bee eats **NECTAR** and gathers pollen from flowers. At the hive, the pollen is fed to larvae and the nectar is turned into honey. Since nectar is 80% water and honey is only 19% water, the bees fan it with their wings for several days until the extra moisture evaporates.
- Most bees are **PASSIVE** unless disturbed. If a bee stings a human, she **DIES**. Since her stinger is barbed, it catches in our skin and rips from her body when she tries to pulls out. A single sting may be fatal to someone who is allergic, but most adults can survive 300 to 500 stings.
- A bee colony is **PERENNIAL** (lasts year after year). A typical hive has 50,000 female workers, 1,000 male drones and only one queen. Workers live for only a few weeks but a queen can live up to four years. The colony stores honey and clusters together for warmth to survive the winter.
- Honeybees build nests (or *combs*) of **WAX**.

BUMBLEBEES are large, furry cousins of the honeybee. Their distinctive buzz comes from beating their wings over 11,000 times per minute. **KILLER BEES** (or Africanized bees) were created in Brazil in 1957 when African honeybees escaped and mated with local bees. They are highly defensive and can stay angry for days. They're no more venomous than other bees but people have died because they weren't able to escape.

THE BUZZ?

WASPS

- Wasps are **SMOOTHER** with bright yellow and black stripes. They have a very small waist.
- Wasps are **CARNIVORES** and eat insects, grubs and spiders. They can bite and also sting (which paralyzes their prey). In wasps that live in large colonies, however, the adults eat fruit and sugar and only the larvae are fed pre-chewed insects.
- Wasps can be very **AGGRESSIVE** if their nest is threatened. Since their stingers have no barbs, they can sting **REPEATEDLY**. Unlike a bee who only defends her colony, a wasp must also sting to catch food.
- A wasp colony is **ANNUAL**. Wasps are divided into workers, drones and queens. In the fall, all the wasps die except for the new queens. They hibernate during winter, then lay eggs in the spring to start new colonies, which can reach up to 15,000 individuals.
- Wasps build **PAPER** nests made from chewed wood fibers. The light gray, oval nests hang from trees or may be buried underground.

Bees and wasps are in different families of the **STINGING** insects. Most live alone but we usually only notice the social ones that live in large colonies. These descriptions are based on honeybees and the hornet/yellowjacket family.

YELLOWJACKETS are common at barbecues, picnics and garbage cans. They're often considered pests but are actually beneficial since they eat many other harmful insects. **HORNETS** are the largest species of wasp.

BROWN BEARS

- The North American brown bear (or **GRIZZLY** bear) once ranged from Alaska to Mexico. Today they only live in the northern parts of the American continent. Kodiak bears (the largest) and the California grizzly (now extinct) are closely related subspecies.
- Grizzlies range from dark brown to cream. Color is influenced by nutrition, shedding and new growth. Their fur tips are lighter in color, giving them a "**GRIZZLED**" or salt-and-pepper look.
- Grizzlies are significantly **LARGER**, although size ranges greatly from 250 to 800 pounds. Influencing factors are gender (males are up to 30% larger), time of year (the feasting or fasting of hibernation) and location (larger along the coasts where food is plentiful).
- Grizzlies have short **ROUNDED** ears, a **CONCAVE** (curving inward) face, and a rump that is **LOWER** than the shoulders. They have a large shoulder hump made of muscle, which provides them with the strength to dig for plant roots and subterranean prey.
- Grizzlies have **DULLER**, **LONGER** claws that are up to four inches long and light in color. Larger claws helps them with digging.

COLOR is not a good indication of who is who. 'Black' bears can be black, bluish-gray, dark brown, light brown, cinnamon, blond and even white. The color range of 'brown' bears is equally as variable. The descriptions here are based on the grizzly bear and the American black bear.

UNBEARABLE!

BLACK BEARS

- The American **BLACK** bear is North America's most widely distributed bear species. The glacier bear (also called the blue bear) is a subspecies in Alaska.
- Black bears **VARY** greatly in color, from pitch black to pure white. Color seems closely tied to region. For example, all bears in the New England area are black, whereas only 50% in the Rocky Mountains and 9% in Yosemite National Park are black. The others are brown or blond.
- Black bears are **SMALLER**, weighing between 200 to 500 pounds.
- Black bears have taller **POINTED** ears, a flat **STRAIGHT** face, and a rump that is **HIGHER** than the shoulders. They lack the distinctive hump of brown bears.
- Black bears have **SHARPER**, **SHORTER** claws that are dark in color and average an inch and a half long. Their claws are curved to help them climb trees, something brown bears can't do because they are so much heavier.

The bear **FAMILY** is divided into three groups: giant pandas, spectacled bears, and all other bears (sloth bears, sun bears, Asian and American black bears, brown bears, polar bears, and even the extinct cave bear). Black bears split off from brown bears and polar bears over five million years ago.

A LITTLE BIRD

SWALLOWS

- Swallows are **SMALLER**.
- Swallows are a dark, glossy **BLUE** color, with a pale underside and red throat.
- Swallows have a longer, **DEEPLY** forked tail. They have shorter, wider, **TRIANGULAR** wings that **FOLD** up while flying.
- Swallows gracefully **GLIDE**, turn and swoop in flight. They flap more slowly and irregularly.
- Swallows generally feed closer to the **GROUND**, often darting over farmland or water.
- Swallows are frequently seen **PERCHING** on wires, fences or branches. During migration time, they gather in flocks.
- Swallow nests are often **VISIBLE**. They build cup-shaped nests in holes, cliffs, porches, barns and under eaves or bridges.
- Swallows have random, chirping, twittering, **BABBLING** songs that aren't very musical.
- Common species are the **BARN SWALLOW** and cliff swallow.

House **MARTINS** and sand martins are in the same family as swallows. Their coloring is slightly different and their tails are much shorter and less forked.

TOLD ME!

SWIFTS

- Swifts are **LARGER**. They have stubby bodies and are often described as a *cigar with wings*.
- Swifts are dark **BROWN** all over, sometimes with a pale throat.
- Swifts have a wider, **SLIGHTLY** forked tail. In some species, the fork is almost absent. They have narrow, **SCYTHE**-shaped wings that are longer than their bodies. Their wings are so **STIFF** (like those of a hummingbird), that they can't bend them while in flight.
- Swifts have **RAPID** wing beats. They rarely fly in a straight line and are similar to bats in terms of their rapid, jerky patterns. They're extremely fast!
- Swifts hunt higher in the **AIR**. They tend to be easier to see in cities than in nature.
- Swifts are almost only seen **FLYING**. Their feet are too weak to perch, although they can cling to vertical surfaces. Some even sleep while flying!
- Swift nests are **HIDDEN** in holes and crevices and never exposed to the outside. Since they can't walk, swifts must be able to swoop directly into their nests.
- Swifts make a shrill, piercing, **SCREAMING** cry while hunting.
- Common types are the **CHIMNEY SWIFT**, Vaux's swift and white-throated swift.

Even though swifts and swallows look very similar, they are not closely **RELATED**. In fact, swifts have more in common with hummingbirds.

WHICH ONE WOULD

FROGS

- Frogs have **SLIM** bodies, **LONG** legs and **SMOOTH** skin. They look moist, silky and delicate and are usually gray or brown in color, but some are also green.
- Frogs are very agile and good at **JUMPING**. Since they rely heavily on their ability to leap (to catch food or escape predators), they have long, powerful legs with heavy, muscular thighs.
- Frogs are good at **SWIMMING**. They're streamlined with large, heavily-webbed back feet.
- Frogs have small, upper **TEETH** but they don't chew their food. The teeth simply prevent their prey from escaping.
- Frogs are found nearly worldwide, but since their skin dries out easily, they mostly live near **WATER**. They are often found in ponds, marshlands, rivers and tropical areas.

TREE FROGS are small with long, skinny hind legs and large toe pads. They're often very bright and can even change color. The color is not for enjoyment but rather for survival. It helps them hide, absorb or reflect light, or warn predators that it is poisonous or distasteful. Poison dart frogs are very dangerous. A single frog may produce 1,900 micrograms of poison. A mere 2 to 200 micrograms are lethal to humans. *So don't kiss this frog!*

YOU RATHER KISS?

TOADS

- Most toads have round, **HEAVY** bodies with **SHORT**, plump back legs. They're covered with dry, rough, **BUMPY** skin and are often brown or gray.
- Toads are not built for speed. They escape by **SECRETING** a thick, whitish fluid from glands in their skin, which can burn the eyes and mouth of a predator. The secretions of some toads can even kill a dog. It's these glands (the so-called *warts*) that give toads their bumpy appearance.
- Toads are good at **DIGGING** and sometimes even have a spade on their foot to dig with.
- Toads **LACK** teeth. They swallow their prey whole.
- Toads can live on **DRY** land because their heavy skin prevents them from drying out. They range from tropical forests to semi-desert areas.

When people started **CLASSIFYING** frogs, they only used two types: a smooth, jumping one and a warty, hopping one. As new species were discovered, they were placed into these two groups based only on superficial characteristics, but that didn't always work. Today there are almost 3,500 species in 21 families. Some families contain both names. For example, *flat-headed frogs* and *fire-bellied toads* are in the same family, as are *midwife toads* and *painted frogs*. All toads are frogs but not all frogs are toads. Think of all tailless amphibians as *frogs* and use *toad* only for those in the true toad family. The differences here are based on the "true" frog and "true" toad families.

ARE THEY STEERING

BISON

- Bison include the **AMERICAN** bison (pictured here) and the slightly taller **EUROPEAN** bison (wisent or auroch). The American bison was once mistakenly called a buffalo by an English naturalist and unfortunately the name stuck, causing endless confusion.
- The American bison lives on the open **PRAIRIES** and grasslands of North America. The European bison lives in the **FORESTS** in central and northern Europe.
- American bison have massive heads and high humped shoulders. Their long, brown **WOOLLY** winter coats fall off in patches in the spring.
- Bison horns are **SEPARATE**, short and curve upward.

Once the dominant animal of the North American prairies, bison almost became **EXTINCT** due to commercial hunting, arrival of the railroads, loss of habitat from ranching and farming, and drought. Their numbers dropped from 30 million in the 1700s to less than 100 in the late 1880s. Fortunately, efforts to repopulate them were successful and current numbers are estimated at 350,000.

YOU WRONG?

BUFFALO

- True buffalo include the **AFRICAN** Cape buffalo (shown here) and the **ASIAN** water buffalo.
- Buffalo are natives of Asia and most parts of Africa. Herds can live in open woodland but prefer high grass or **THICKETS** for cover. They like areas close to **WATER** or swampy ground where they can wallow.
- African buffalo have a broad chest and large, droopy ears. They only have **SPARSE** hair.
- Buffalo horns are **JOINED** at the base and cover the animal's forehead like a helmet. They then spread out and downward, or upward, or out and back (depending on the species).

The **BOVIDAE** family includes bison, buffalo, oxen, antelopes, gazelles, cattle, sheep and goats. Subfamilies include similar-looking animals such as the muskox, yak, wildebeest (or gnu) and gaur (largest of the Asiatic cattle).

OCTOPUSES

- Octopuses have a large, **ROUND** head and **EIGHT** arms (not tentacles), each covered with one or two rows of suckers along most of its length.
- Octopuses are completely **SOFT**. They have no hard shell or bones. This allows them to squeeze into tight spaces and small gaps.
- Octopuses are **SMALLER**, ranging from a mere half inch in length (and one-thirtieth of an ounce in weight) to over 16 feet long and almost 600 pounds.
- Octopuses are **SOLITARY**, living alone on the **SEA FLOOR** in dens such as rock crevices, holes they dug, or even old bottles. The den protects them from predators such as moray eels.
- Octopuses feed on bottom-dwelling **CRUSTACEANS** (crab, shrimp), snails, and even other octopuses. They capture their prey with their arms, inject it with a paralyzing nerve venom, then **SUCK** out the meat that has been dissolved by their saliva. Only the Australian blue-ringed octopus has venom strong enough to kill a human.

The **WORD** octopus, coined by biologist Carl Linnaeus in the 1700s, combines both Latin and Greek, with octo (eight) and pus (foot). In all Latin, it would be octopede (think of centipede), while the ancient Greeks named the animal a polypous (many-footed). As such, people have often been confused about the plural. In Greek it would be octopodes; in Latin it's octopi, and in English, octopuses. Today, octopuses is generally accepted as being correct.

TWIST THEIR ARMS!

SQUID

- Squid have an **ELONGATED** body, triangular-shaped head, and **TEN** appendages (eight arms and two long tentacles). Tentacles only have suckers at the tips. Some may also have hooks. Squid have two head fins.
- Squid have a **STIFF** structure (called a *pen*), which acts like a flexible backbone. This helps stabilize them while swimming.
- While also having a wide range of sizes, squid can be much **LARGER**. The colossal squid lives over 7,200 feet deep. It can grow over 40 feet long and weigh up to 1,600 pounds.
- Some squid live in large **SCHOOLS** when they are young and become solitary when older. They swim in the **OPEN** ocean.
- Squid eat **FISH** and shrimp, which they catch with their specialized tentacles. They then **TEAR** their prey apart, consuming it in chunks. They must be fast, not only to catch their food but to escape predators such as sharks, whales and other squid.

Octopuses, squid, cuttlefish and nautiluses are **CEPHALOPODS** (meaning *head-footed*). They belong to a larger group called mollusks (from the Latin *mollusca* meaning soft), which also include snails and clams. Nautiluses have kept the hard, protective, external shell; cuttlefish have a hard internal shell (cuttlebone); squid have a soft internal shell, and octopuses have lost the shell completely. Calamari are a smaller species of squid.

POSSUMS

- Possums live in **AUSTRALIA**, New Guinea and Eastern Indonesia. The common brushtail possum (described here) is one of the larger species.
- Possums are **SMALLER**. They're one to two feet long (with an extra foot of tail) and weigh two to ten pounds.
- Possums have **SOFT** fur. Their coats can be silver-gray, brown, black or gold.
- Possums have a **BUSHY** tail and ears. The tip of the tail is prehensile, meaning it's capable of grasping. They can hold onto branches with it as if it were another hand. They also use it to carry nesting materials such as grass.
- Possums mainly feed on **LEAVES** but also consume flowers, fruit, ferns, bark, sap, snails, bird eggs and even carrion.
- Possums live **LONGER**, up to five or six years.

Marsupials are divided into American (opossums) and Australian (kangaroos, koalas, wombats, possums, sugar gliders) groups. The **WORD** *opossum* was first recorded by English colonists in America in the early 1600s. It comes from a Powhatan word meaning *white animal.* The slang quickly became *possum,* which was then carried to Australia in 1770 on Captain James Cook's ship, the Endeavour, and applied to the similar-looking marsupials there.

PLAYING POSSUM?

OPOSSUMS

- Opossums live in the **AMERICAS**. Originating in South America, they eventually migrated north. They vary drastically in size and appearance. The Virginia opossum (described here) is the only marsupial in North America.
- Opossums vary greatly in size, being much bigger in the north. The **LARGER** opossums can be over three feet long (plus another foot and a half for the tail) and weigh up to 14 pounds.
- Opossums have **COARSE** fur. They have a white face and grayish-white body.
- Opossums have a **BALD** tail and ears. They can use their prehensile tails for climbing and holding objects, but only juveniles can actually hang briefly from them. Adults are too heavy.
- Opossums eat **EVERYTHING**… grass, berries, insects, crayfish, lizards, frogs, mice, eggs, young rabbits and even venomous snakes! Their very sharp teeth can make them look quite scary.
- Opossums have a **SHORTER** lifespan of only two to four years.

Since opossums can't run quickly, they have a different defensive **STRATEGY**… they mimic the appearance and smell of a dead animal. They slow their heartbeat, become stiff, emit a foul musk and foam at the mouth. This involuntary response kicks in after all other options of escape have been tried. They can stay like this for a few minutes or several hours. Even if the predator bites, the opossum won't move. Fortunately they have an exceptional healing ability.

SOMETHING ABOUT
OLD WORLD VULTURES

- Old World vultures live in **EUROPE**, **AFRICA** and **ASIA**. They prefer drier, warmer and more open areas.
- This group includes the **GRIFFON VULTURE**, cinereous vulture and Himalayan vulture.
- Old World vultures use **SIGHT** to find their food, which consists of dead animals. Vultures rarely kill anything. Their beaks and talons are not strong enough. Sometimes they can't even break into a carcass and have to wait for a stronger bird or animal to do it for them.
- Old World vultures have a **VOICE BOX** and can make a wide variety of calls and noises.
- Old World vultures can't run very well but will **HOP** or flap for short distances when necessary.
- Old World vultures build **NESTS** from sticks and leaves in trees or on cliffs. They may use the same nest for several years.

Until about 25 years ago, a vulture was a vulture. It was then discovered that American vultures were quite **DIFFERENT**. The similarities are due to convergent evolution, with both groups serving as environmental clean-up crews. Old World vultures are in the same family as hawks and eagles. New World vultures are in their own group. Some ornithologists believe they're more closely related to storks or herons than birds of prey.

THIS SMELLS FUNNY!
NEW WORLD VULTURES

- New World vultures reside in North, Central, and South **AMERICA**. They have a wide range of habitats, including high mountain peaks, deserts and tropical rainforests.
- This group includes the **TURKEY VULTURE**, black vulture and condor.
- New World vultures find decaying carcasses using their sense of **SMELL**. They can detect a rotting animal up to a mile away.
- New World Vultures lack a voice box, so they can only **HISS** and grunt. Many are silent most of the time.
- New World Vultures are able to **RUN**, much like a chicken does.
- New World Vultures don't build nests. They lay their eggs in **PROTECTED** locations such as in hollow logs, caves, crevices or on the ground in a thicket.

In much of North America, a **BUZZARD** refers to the turkey vulture (a New World vulture). Think of them circling in those old Western movies! Elsewhere in the world, a buzzard is a hawk in the *Buteo* genus (in the Old World vulture family). This confusion probably dates back to the time of the English colonists, who had seen hawks but never a vulture, much in the same way the bison was mistakenly called a buffalo.

IT'S THE LITTLE

ANTS

- **WORKERS** are all small, wingless, sterile females. They care for the others, dig tunnels, and search for food outside the nest.
- **SOLDIERS** are larger, stronger and have powerful jaws. They too are all sterile females. They protect the colony and help carry large objects.
- **ALATES** are fertile males (*drones*) and females (*queens*) born with large wings. In summer, they fly off to form their own colonies. After mating, the drone dies and the queen begins laying millions of eggs, which will become her workers, drones and future queens. When she dies (about 30 years), the colony dies too.
- Ants have **FOUR** stages of development (complete metamorphosis): egg, larva, pupa, adult. When the eggs hatch, the baby ants (larva) look like small worms. They eat and grow rapidly. In the pupal stage, they transform into an adult (like a caterpillar to a butterfly).
- Ants are **DARKER** in color, ranging from red to black. They have a **THIN** waist and three distinct sections: head, thorax and abdomen. They have segmented, **BENT** antennae.
- Alates have **DIFFERENT**-sized wings. Their hind wings are shorter and smaller.
- Ants are **OMNIVORES** and scavengers, eating almost anything.

Both ants and termites have different **CASTES** (groups) based on their roles in the colony. Details can vary drastically depending on the species. For example with ants, some don't have soldiers; some have winged workers; some workers can lay eggs (but can't produce a fertile adult), or they can have a single queen, several queens or no queen at all.

THINGS THAT COUNT!

TERMITES

- **WORKERS** are small, wingless, permanently immature males and females. They never leave the underground colony and are blind with soft bodies.
- **SOLDIERS** are like workers but with large, hard heads. They stand guard at the nest entrances but can't do much else. Their jaws are so large that they need help being fed.
- **ALATES** are the only termites with eyes, wings and hard bodies. After a colony matures, the fertile males (*kings*) and females (*queens*) leave in a big swarm. A pair burrows into the ground and lives inside a royal chamber until they die (up to 50 years). She lays over 1,000 eggs a day and has secondary queens producing eggs nearby. When the queen dies, a new one takes over.
- Termites undergo **THREE** stages of development (incomplete metamorphosis): egg, nymph, adult. The baby termite (nymph) looks like a young adult, which then grows to full size.
- Termites are **LIGHT** in color or even transparent. They have a **THICK** body with no waist, making it look like they only have two sections. They have beaded, **STRAIGHT** antennae.
- Alates have **EQUAL**-sized wings that are longer than their bodies.
- Termites eat **CELLULOSE**, a material in wood and plants. They're also detritivores, consuming dead plant material, leaf litter and soil.

Termites are more closely **RELATED** to cockroaches than ants. They branched off from a common ancestor about 100 million years ago. Ants are more closely related to bees, evolving from a wasp-like ancestor about 140 million years ago. They diversified after the rise of flowering plants.

DROMEDARIES

- The dromedary or **ARABIAN** camel has **ONE** hump. There are dozens of words for *camel* in Arabic. While *dromedary* actually only refers to one specific type of racing camel, the word is now applied to all one-humped camels.
- Dromedaries live in dry regions of the **MIDDLE EAST** and in parts of **AFRICA**, including the Sahara Desert. There are no longer any dromedaries in the wild.
- Dromedaries were domesticated about **4,000 YEARS** ago. They transport people and goods and are a source of milk, meat, wool and leather. This enables people to live in otherwise uninhabitable areas.
- Dromedaries have smoother, **SHORTER** hair. They live in temperatures from 30°F in winter to 150°F in summer. Colors range from cream to almost black.
- Dromedaries are typically **TALLER** at the hump.

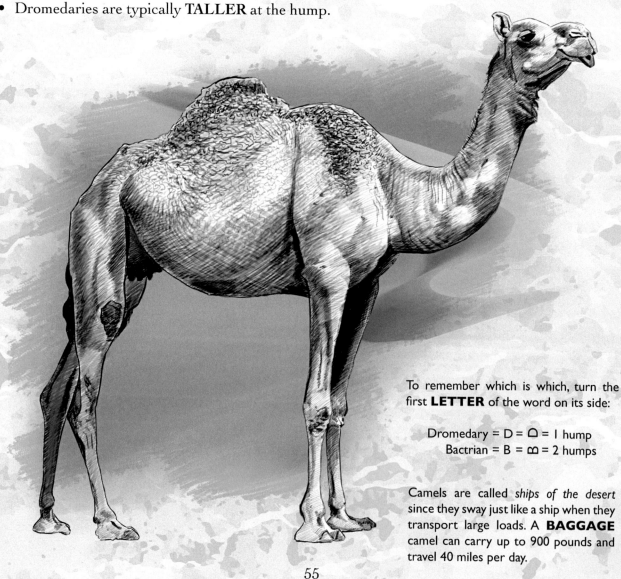

To remember which is which, turn the first **LETTER** of the word on its side:

Dromedary = D = ◠ = 1 hump
Bactrian = B = ◠◠ = 2 humps

Camels are called *ships of the desert* since they sway just like a ship when they transport large loads. A **BAGGAGE** camel can carry up to 900 pounds and travel 40 miles per day.

OR TWO?

BACTRIAN CAMELS

- The Bactrian or **ASIAN** camel has **TWO** humps. Bactria was a province in the old Persian Empire (currently Afghanistan).
- Bactrian camels live on the dry steppes of the **GOBI** desert (Mongolia and China). Most of them are domesticated, with less than 1,000 camels in the wild. These are considered endangered.
- Bactrian camels were domesticated **3,000 YEARS** ago. They are sturdier and can transport heavier loads. They can outrun a horse and carry three times as much.
- Bactrian camels have **LONGER** hair, especially in winter. They live in cooler, rockier regions with extreme temperatures (-20°F in winter to 140°F in summer). In spring, they shed their shaggy coats very rapidly in large patches.
- They have **SHORTER** legs, a heavier build and harder feet.

HUMPS are made of fat, which can be used as food or converted to water. Hump size varies with the camel's health. When there is no food, the hump shrinks or even flops over.

Camels can go several days without **WATER** and lose 25% of their body weight without any problems (other animals die at 15% body weight loss). They can drink 30 gallons of water in just 10 minutes! They store it in their stomachs, not their humps.

LET'S SHED A RAY

STINGRAYS

- Stingrays are **SMALLER**, the largest being about 14 feet long. They can weigh up to 800 pounds. They're **LONGER** than they are wide.
- Stingrays can be found in a **VARIETY** of temperatures, including tropical, subtropical and even temperate. They live in **BOTH** saltwater and freshwater.
- Most stingrays are **DEMERSAL**, dwelling close to the ocean floor.
- Stingrays have mouths on the **UNDERSIDE** of their bodies. This is because they're **BOTTOM FEEDERS**, digging up crustaceans and mollusks buried in the sand.
- Stingrays have colors that match the **SEAFLOOR**. Sometimes they will even partially bury themselves in the sand.
- Stingrays have one or more barbed **STINGERS** on their tail. These are only used in self defense. Most also have venom glands, which inject a painful toxin.

Both rays are cartilaginous **FISH** that are related to sharks. Closer relatives include devil rays, electric rays, eagle rays, skates, wedgefish, guitarfish and sawfish.

OF LIGHT ON THINGS!

MANTA RAYS

- Manta rays are **LARGER**, reaching 25 feet wide and weighing over 3,000 pounds. They are **WIDER** than they are long.
- Manta rays live mostly in **WARM**, tropical and subtropical **SALTWATER** locations.
- Manta rays are exclusively **PELAGIC**, meaning they live in the upper layers of the open sea.
- Manta rays have mouths in **FRONT** of their bodies since they are **FILTER FEEDERS**. As they swim, they swallow large amounts of water filled with zooplankton. A pair of large horn-like fins on their heads help funnel food into their mouths. Special gill rakers then strain or *filter* out the plankton. These gills are regularly cleaned by other fish such as remoras.
- Manta rays are typically dark on top and light underneath. This helps them blend in with the **WATER**.
- Manta rays **LACK** a tail stinger.

All manta rays are stingrays but not all stingrays are manta rays. A manta ray is technically a **TYPE** of stingray that's lost its sting.

CARIBOU

- Caribou are **WILD** reindeer. Attempts have been made, but they've never been domesticated.
- Caribou live in the circumpolar regions of **NORTH AMERICA**, including Alaska, Canada and Greenland. This includes Arctic, taiga (subarctic or *boreal* forests) and tundra landscapes.
- Caribou **MIGRATE** long distances. Each year, they travel over 3,000 miles. In the summer, they head north to feed on the abundant plants of the tundra. When the first snow falls, they return south to overwinter in the sheltering mountains.
- Caribou are **LARGER** (with longer legs) and their fur is **THINNER** and less dense. These adaptations help with their long migrations and their following of the seasons.
- Caribou calves are born in **MAY**. Within a few hours, newborns can follow their mothers at speeds of 45 miles per hour!
- When chased, caribou tend to **SCATTER**.
- Female caribou have **SMALLER** antlers than female reindeer do. In other deer species, only the males grow antlers.

Deer are divided into Old World (elk/wapati, fallow deer) and New World deer (reindeer, moose, white-tailed deer) based on their ankle structure and where they originated. Reindeer and caribou are the **SAME** species but different subspecies. It's similar to how the pet dog is a subspecies of the wolf and has changed over time through domestication. In North America, wild reindeer are called *caribou*. Elsewhere, people use *wild* versus *domesticated* reindeer.

DEER!

REINDEER

- Reindeer were **DOMESTICATED** around 2,000 years ago in northern Eurasia. There are still some wild populations left, but mostly they are herded by many Arctic peoples in Europe and Asia who depend on them for food, clothing and shelter.
- Reindeer live in the circumpolar regions of **EURASIA**, including Siberia and Scandinavia.
- Reindeer are more **SEDENTARY**. They're herded between grazing ranges but never very far.
- Reindeer are **SHORTER** and stouter. They have **THICK**, dense fur. Since they are not given the freedom to follow the seasons, they must be able to survive all types of weather.
- Reindeer calves are born in **APRIL**.
- When chased or herded, reindeer will cluster **TOGETHER**.
- Female reindeer have **LARGER** antlers than female caribou. Males shed their antlers in the winter while most females keep theirs until spring.

Reindeer were first mentioned pulling **SANTA'S** sleigh in 1823. But since most male reindeer have shed their antlers by Christmas, this means they were probably female! Rudolph the Red-nosed Reindeer was introduced in 1939. In order to breathe cold air, reindeer noses heat up the air with a dense network of blood vessels carrying red, oxygen-rich blood… truly creating a red nose!

60

LOBSTERS

- Lobsters live in **SALTWATER**, mostly in the ocean but occasionally in brackish water.
- Lobsters can live up to **70 YEARS**. Since they never stop growing, this long length of time allows them to reach **LARGER** sizes. On average they are ten to 20 inches long, but some species reach over three feet long and weigh over 40 pounds.
- Lobsters have an **ELONGATED** body, muscular tail and very long antennae.
- Lobsters have claws on their first **THREE** sets of legs, but only the first pair is very large.
- Lobsters walk slowly **FORWARD** along the seafloor. If they need to flee quickly, they can swim backwards up to 11 miles per hour.
- Lobsters are **SOLITARY**. They live alone, hidden under rocks or in burrows on the sea floor.

Although many crustaceans are **NAMED** *lobster*, the term is generally meant for clawed lobsters (described here), which include the American and European lobster. Their closest relatives are reef lobsters and crayfish (a kind of freshwater lobster). Horseshoe crabs look like crustaceans but are actually closely related to spiders.

IN A PINCH?

CRABS

- Crabs live in a **VARIETY** of environments, primarily in the sea but also in fresh water and on land, especially in tropical regions.
- Crabs live up to **13 YEARS**. Overall, they're **SMALLER** but can range from a few millimeters wide (pea crab) up to a 13-foot leg span (Japanese spider crab).
- Crabs are **ROUND** with long eyestalks. Their small tails and antennae are almost unnoticeable.
- Crabs have claws only on their **FIRST** set of legs. In males, sometimes one claw is much larger than the other.
- Most crabs walk **SIDEWAYS**. Because their shells restrict the motion of their upper joints, their lower joints have adapted to bend only sideways. Some crabs with wider shells can walk forwards.
- Crabs are **SOCIAL**. They work together to collect food and protect their families. However, they can often get into fights over territories and mating partners.

DECAPODS (meaning *ten-footed*) are a type of crustacean. Classification depends on the gills, legs and how the larvae develop. The main groups are:

- Clawed lobsters, crayfish
- True crabs (depicted here)
- Shrimps, prawns
- Clawless lobsters (spiny, rock, slipper and furry lobsters)
- Hermit, king, porcelain and coconut crabs, sand fleas, squat lobsters

WHOSE BIRD-BRAINED

OSTRICHES

- Ostriches live in **AFRICA**.
- Ostriches are the **LARGEST** bird in the world. They grow up to nine feet tall and weigh 250 to 400 pounds. They have a life span of 40 to 50 years.
- Male and female ostriches are **DIFFERENT** colors. Males are black and white while females are grayish brown. The males are larger in size.
- Ostriches have **TWO** toes per foot. They can run over 40 miles per hour. That's faster than a horse!
- Ostrich eggs are **WHITE**, round, nearly six inches long and weigh up to four pounds. They have a very thick shell.
- Ostriches form **GROUPS** during the breeding season, with one male mating with six or seven females. All the females lay their eggs in the same nest. The eggs are incubated (kept warm) by the females during the day and the male at night. This provides a natural camouflage.
- Ostriches are raised for their **FEATHERS**, meat and leather. The feathers were fashionable in the late 1800s for military uniforms and women's hats.

Ostriches have eyes larger than their brains (which is about the size of a walnut). So while they aren't very intelligent, they are smart enough *not* to **BURY** their heads in the sand (since they'd suffocate). It only *looks* like they do because their nests are dug in shallow holes and they turn their eggs over with their beaks several times a day.

IDEA WAS THIS?

EMUS

- Emus live in **AUSTRALIA**.
- Emus are **SMALLER**, growing up to six feet tall and weighing 90 to 150 pounds. They live 20 to 30 years.
- Male and female emus have the **SAME** color, a deep brown. During breeding season, the females develop black feathers and blue patches on their heads. Females are larger than males.
- Emus have **THREE** toes per foot and can reach speeds of 30 miles per hour.
- Emu eggs are **GREENISH-BLUE**, oblong, five inches long and weigh about one and a half pounds. They have thin shells.
- Emus form **PAIRS** during the mating season. After the female lays the eggs, the male sits on them until they hatch, going without food or water for 56 days. Meanwhile, the female looks for another mate. Once the chicks hatch, they stay with their father for six months.
- Emus are raised for their **OIL**, meat and eggs. The oil is used in medicinal and cosmetic items.

Emus and ostriches belong to a group of flightless birds called **RATITES**. Their relatives are the cassowaries in New Guinea and Indonesia and the rheas in South America. How did such similar birds end up different continents?

One theory is that they shared a flightless ancestor millions of years ago on the supercontinent of Gondwana and were separated as it broke up. Another is that their small ancestors could fly long distances. Once they found a safe place to live, they lost their ability to fly. Some stayed small like kiwis, and others grew huge like the extinct moa.

MICE

- Pet mice descend from the **HOUSE MOUSE**, which originally came from Asia on trade ships. The earliest domesticated mice were kept in the royal palaces of Japan and China.
- Mice have **SMALL** slender bodies. They're under three inches long excluding the tail (which is often **LONGER** than their bodies) and they weigh less than one ounce. Mice can squeeze through openings a quarter inch in diameter.
- Mice have a **POINTED** nose and relatively **LARGE** ears, which would cover their eyes if you were to pull them down.
- Mice have **SMOOTH** fur that is light brown or dusty gray on top and cream underneath. Males have a distinctive odor due to musk glands, which rats don't have.
- Mice are relatively **TIMID** and won't venture too far from their nests. Indoors, they prefer walls, rafters, **ATTICS** and ceilings, although any place with an ample food supply will do.
- Mice live in groups but the males are highly **TERRITORIAL**. They only allow a family group of several females and their young to live in their area.

With thousands of different types, **RODENTS** comprise almost half of all mammal species. They're divided into three main groups:

- Squirrels, beavers, marmots
- Porcupines, chinchillas, guinea pigs
- Rats, mice, voles, lemmings, hamsters, gerbils, jerboas, muskrats

Since black rats (roof or ship rats) are very similar to mice, characteristics of the larger brown rat (Norway rat) are described here.

CHEESE!

RATS

- Pet rats descend from the **BROWN RAT**. It too originally came from Asia but is now found worldwide after stowing away on European ships during the 16th to 18th centuries.
- Rats are **LARGER** and stockier, with a body length of up to almost ten inches. The tail is **SHORTER** than the body. Rats generally weigh one to two pounds.
- Rats have a **BLUNT** nose and **SMALL** close-set ears.
- Rats have **COARSE** shaggy fur. They're generally brown in color with a beige underside.
- Rats like to **EXPLORE** but they are still cautious with new objects. Indoors, they prefer the **LOWER** floors of buildings but also aren't too picky as long as food is involved.
- Rats live in large **GROUPS** (called a *mischief*) and will aggressively defend their group against outsiders.

Why are they always **CHEWING** on things? Rats and mice have long incisor teeth, which grow continuously throughout their lives. They must wear these down by constantly grinding or gnawing, otherwise their teeth would grow into their lips.

BOAS

- Boas are **OVOVIVIPAROUS**, meaning the eggs inside the female are surrounded by a membrane instead of a hard shell. When boa babies are born, they break through this membrane and crawl out of their mother. It's almost like having live young.
- Boas are primarily found in the **NEW WORLD**. Most live in South and Central America but some smaller species live in Africa, western Asia, Madagascar and some Pacific islands. They live mainly in tropical areas and can be terrestrial, tree-dwelling or burrowing. Some are brightly colored like the emerald tree boa or the rainbow boa.
- The **BOA CONSTRICTOR** lives in the rainforests of South America. It can be 12 feet long and weigh 30 pounds. The South American **ANACONDA** is the largest boa, reaching 30 feet in length, three feet in girth and weighing over 350 pounds. It lives in swamps and shallow rivers and eats birds, fish, turtles, deer, reptiles, caimans and even jaguars!

Boas and pythons are members of the same family but belong to different **SUBFAMILIES**. They are considered primitive snakes (among the first snakes to evolve) and still have features that link them to lizards.

OR MISS?

PYTHONS

- Pythons are **OVIPAROUS**. This means the eggs are surrounded by a thin shell. A python lays her eggs and coils around them for the six to eight week incubation period. She uses muscular contractions to keep them several degrees above that of the surrounding air. In both pythons and boas, the young are immediately self-sufficient.
- Pythons are mostly found in the **OLD WORLD** tropics of Africa, Asia, Australia and the South Pacific islands, but there's also a species in Central America. They can't survive in temperatures below 77°F.
- The **RETICULATED PYTHON** lives in southeast Asia, Indonesia and the Philippines. It can reach 30 feet in length and weigh over 200 pounds. The **BURMESE PYTHON** ranges from India to lower China and reaches lengths of over 20 feet.

They both kill by **CONSTRICTION** (wrapping around and crushing their prey). They have teeth which are used to hold onto their prey to prevent it from escaping, but they are not venomous.

WOLVES

- Wolves are **LARGER**. Size varies depending on location (the largest live in Canada), but in general, they weigh around 75 pounds.
- Wolves have **ROUND** ears and a square snout. Colors are white, cream, gray, brown and black.
- Wolves eat **FRESH** meat. They prefer larger animals such as **DEER** and elk but will also eat rabbits and beavers. They can eat up to 20 pounds of meat at one time and swallow their food in large chunks without chewing so they can regurgitate it later for hungry pups.
- Wolves hunt in **PACKS** of up to 30 members. They mostly attack young, old, sick or weak animals. In desert areas where prey is smaller, packs may only have a few members.
- Wolves raise their pups in a den made from a **NATURAL** hole or burrow. Only the dominant (or *alpha*) pair will have pups but the entire pack will care for them. Young wolves may **STAY** with the pack for several years before moving on.

The **DOG** family includes jackals, coyotes, wolves, foxes, dingos, and all breeds of dogs. There are many wolf subspecies such as the Mexican wolf and the Arctic wolf. Extinct European wolves are possibly the ancestor of the domestic dog, which evolved over 20,000 years ago.

CRYING WOLF?

COYOTES

- Coyotes are **SMALLER**. They weigh around 35 pounds, although desert coyotes tend to weigh less than mountain coyotes.
- Coyotes have **POINTED** ears and snouts. Most are gray but some have rust or brown colors.
- Coyotes are often **SCAVENGERS**, eating whatever they can find. Their diet includes fresh and spoiled meat, fish, **RABBITS**, squirrels, mice, insects, reptiles, fruits, berries and even grasses.
- Coyotes hunt **ALONE** but may gather in pairs or small groups to hunt larger animals such as young deer. They're mostly active at night but will also hunt during the day.
- Coyotes **DIG** their own dens or might enlarge an old badger hole. Coyotes mate for life. The female selects her partner and allows him to help support the family with regurgitated food, but he's not allowed to enter the den. The young **LEAVE** to find their own territories in the fall.

Wolves and coyotes don't **SHARE** territories. Wolves will chase and even kill coyotes. Coyotes, however, can breed successfully with both wolves and domestic dogs. A dog/coyote pup is called a *coydog*.

ANTEATERS

- The **THREE** types are the giant anteater (described here), collared anteater (tamandua) and silky anteater.
- Anteaters live in tropical savannas and forests in Central and South **AMERICA**.
- Anteaters are **TOOTHLESS**. They use their long snouts and even longer sticky tongues (up to two feet!) to catch termites and ants. Digestion is aided by pebbles they swallow while eating. A giant anteater can eat 30,000 insects per day and flick its tongue up to 160 times per minute.
- Anteater have long, coarse **HAIR**, a bushy tail and a tube-shaped head. Adults can get up to eight feet long (half of that is the tail) and weigh up to 140 pounds.
- Anteaters spend the **DAY** looking for food. At night they sleep in hollow logs or empty burrows. They can cover themselves with their own tails to keep warm.
- A mother anteater **CARRIES** her single offspring on her back for a long time, even long after it can walk by itself.

The anteater, aardvark, spiny anteater (echidna), scaly anteater (pangolin) and banded anteater (numbat) are completely **UNRELATED**. In fact, the closest relatives to anteaters are sloths and armadillos. The closest relative to the spiny anteater is the platypus. The banded anteater is a marsupial, and the aardvark is the last surviving member of an ancient line of hoofed mammals and has no close relatives at all.

OF THEIR TONGUES!

AARDVARKS

- There's only **ONE** type of aardvark, which means *earth pig* in Afrikaans (a language in South Africa). It's also called an antbear.
- Aardvarks are found in sub-Sahara **AFRICA**. They live in savannas, grasslands and forests.
- Aardvarks have **CYLINDRICAL TEETH** towards the back of the jaw. These are rootless and never stop growing. Aardvarks follow established pathways between termite nests, sweeping the ground with their noses and walking in a zigzag fashion. They also have sticky tongues.
- Aardvarks have stocky bodies and thick, grayish-brown **SKIN** with sparse, coarse hair. They can reach five feet long (not including the tail) and weigh up to 175 pounds.
- Aardvarks are **NOCTURNAL**. During the day, they sleep in a tight ball in extensive burrows that they dig. On average they'll use a burrow for one week before moving on.
- An aardvark baby will remain in the **BURROW** for its first two weeks and start eating termites at nine weeks old. It starts digging burrows at six months but will remain with its mother for a year.

Aardvarks **LOOK** as if they were stitched together from many animals. They have a pig-like nose, large rabbit-like ears and a strong kangaroo-like tail.

LET'S JUST CHUCK

MARMOTS

- The yellow-bellied marmot (described here) is a species of **PETROMARMOTA** (Greek *petros* meaning rock).
- Yellow-bellied marmots have the nickname **ROCK CHUCKS**. All marmots are also called *whistle pigs* due to their plump shape and the high-pitched whistles they use to signal danger.
- Marmots are found in the **WESTERN** United States and into southern Canada.
- Marmots weigh slightly **LESS**, with an average of eight pounds. They have a **VARIED** coat, with a frosty brown body and head, a yellow-orange underside and white face patches.
- Marmots live in the **MOUNTAINS**, such as the Rocky Mountains and Sierra Nevadas. They prefer open areas with low-growing or sparse vegetation. Those at high elevations may hibernate over half their lives, huddling close together in a burrow room insulated with dried grass.
- Marmots will establish their burrows within **ROCK PILES** if the ground is too hard to dig.
- Marmots are highly **SOCIAL** and often live in colonies of up to 20 individuals.
- Marmots can live up to **FIFTEEN** years in the wild.

Marmots, the largest members of the squirrel family, are divided into two **SUBGROUPS**:

- Marmota: European and Asian marmots, plus two in North America (Alaska marmots, groundhogs)
- Petromarmota: western North American marmots (hoary marmots, yellow-bellied marmots)

73

THE WHOLE THING!

GROUNDHOGS

- The groundhog is a species of **MARMOTA**.
- A groundhog is also called a **WOODCHUCK**. *How much wood would a woodchuck chuck if a woodchuck could chuck wood?* Woodchucks actually have nothing to do with wood. The name evolved from Native American words, such as *wuchak*, *weijack* or *otchek*.
- Groundhogs are found throughout the **EASTERN** United States, across Canada, and into parts of Alaska.
- Groundhogs weigh **MORE**, up to 13 pounds. They have a **SOLID** brown coat that can be light, dark, reddish or grayish.
- Groundhogs are **LOWLAND** animals, living in low elevation forests and fields.
- Groundhogs **DIG** extensive burrows in the ground with multiple entrances and side rooms. Most have summer and winter dens.
- Groundhogs are **SOLITARY** and territorial.
- Groundhogs live four to **SIX** years in the wild (up to ten years in captivity).

GROUNDHOG DAY has been European folklore for centuries (although they used hedgehogs and badgers). German settlers brought the tradition with them to the American colonies but had to use a different animal. Supposedly, on February 2nd, if a groundhog emerges from its burrow after its long hibernation and sees its shadow, it will retreat and winter will last six more weeks. If it is shadowless due to a cloudy day, it takes it as a sign of spring and remains above ground.

HORSES

- Horses are **LARGER**, with shorter, thinner ears, longer faces and narrower foreheads. Their manes and long tails are soft and flowing, with separate strands of hair. Their larger hooves are more oval and angled.
- Horses prefer **HERDS** and larger groups.
- Horses have a strong flight response and will quickly **RUN** from any perceived danger.
- Horses talk in smooth **WHINNIES** and neighs.
- Horses are used for **TRANSPORTATION**, carrying people quickly and for long distances.
- The **PRZEWALSKI'S HORSE** on the Mongolian steppe is the only remaining true wild horse in the world. Wild mustangs, on the other hand, are descended from domesticated horses that escaped. Horses were domesticated some 5,500 years ago.

A **PONY** is not just a short horse. Ponies have heavier bones, shorter legs, wider chests, thicker necks, shorter heads, and thicker manes and coats that protect them from the cold. Short horses that don't have pony characteristics include the Icelandic horse.

NEIGH-SAYERS!

DONKEYS

- Donkeys are **SHORTER** and sturdier, with long, thick ears. Their manes are stiff and bristly, and their thin tails look more like a cow's, with coarse hair on the lower part. Their smaller hooves are more upright and box-shaped.
- Donkeys are less social and tend to form a strong bond with only **ONE** other donkey.
- Donkeys are harder to startle but will **FREEZE** up when scared. This reaction has given them their reputation for being stubborn.
- Donkeys bray with a distinctive **HEE-HAW** sound.
- Donkeys are primarily used as working and **PACK** animals. They lack the speed of a horse but are good for hard labor, especially in areas with little water. Their backs are flatter and can't hold a normal saddle.
- Originating in Africa, the **WILD ASS** was domesticated around 4,000 BC. They arrived in the Americas along with Christopher Columbus in 1495.

A donkey, **BURRO** and ass are all the same animal. Sometime in the 1700s, the word *donkey* replaced *ass*, with a *jack* being a male and a *jenny* being a female. *Burro* is the Spanish word for the animal. A **MULE** is produced when a male donkey is bred with a female horse. A *hinny* comes from a male horse and a female donkey. Mules are sterile and unable to reproduce. They tend to be larger than donkeys but with a more delicate bone structure.

SEALS

- Seals have no external ear flaps, although their **EAR HOLES** are sometimes visible.
- Seals have **SHORT**, blunt front flippers with **CLAWS**.
- A seal's hind flippers are important for swimming but can't be used for walking. Seals **CRAWL** on land by dragging their rear flippers or moving forward like an inchworm.
- The **ELEPHANT SEAL** is the largest seal, measuring up to 20 feet long and weighing up to four tons. It can dive to a depth of one mile and remain underwater for two hours. Seals are found at all latitudes, from the Arctic **HARP SEAL** (once hunted for its fur) to the **MONK SEAL** (the only tropical seal) to the Weddell seal (the world's southernmost mammal).

Marine mammals known as **PINNIPEDS** (Latin meaning *fin-footed*) include earless or true seals, eared seals (sea lions and fur seals) and walruses. Earless seals are believed to have descended from an otter-like land mammal, whereas eared seals probably descended from a bear-like mammal.

ARE SEALED!

SEA LIONS

- Sea lions have small external **EAR FLAPS**.
- Sea lions have **LONG**, wing-like, **CLAWLESS** front flippers for swimming or rowing through the water.
- A sea lion's paddle-like hind flippers can be rotated forward beneath the body so sea lions can **WALK** on land on all four flippers.
- Almost all sea lions live in the southern oceans. The **CALIFORNIA SEA LION** is one of the few who lives on both sides of the Equator. The **NORTHERN SEA LION** is the largest, weighing up to one ton. **FUR SEALS** are actually a type of sea lion. Their warm fur replaces the thick layer of blubber found in other sea lions and seals.

When you see a **TRAINED** seal at the zoo, you are most likely seeing a trained sea lion. Sea lions quickly learn new tricks and move easier on land. The California sea lion is the most common performing pinniped.

DUCKS

- Ducks are **SMALLER**, with shorter necks, stouter bodies and shorter legs. Their lifespan is usually five to ten years.
- Ducks are usually **BRIGHTLY** colored.
- Males and females are very **DIFFERENT** in appearance. The males are colorful while the females are dull brown colors.
- Most ducks eat **FISH**, worms, insects and some vegetable matter. They have different bills depending on their diet. Some are *diving* ducks whereas other are *dabbling* ducks (feeding on the water's surface and on land).
- Ducks mate only for a **SEASON**. After the eggs hatch, the males leave and the females raise the ducklings.
- Ducks were **DOMESTICATED** for eggs, meat and feathers (called *down*) by the ancient Chinese and Maya. Some can still fly but others have been bred with heavy bodies and small wings.

Technically, the word *duck* only refers to the female. The male is a *drake*. Likewise, *goose* is the female and *gander* is the male.

79

WILD GOOSE CHASE!

GEESE

- Geese are **LARGER** than ducks but smaller than swans. They have shorter bills and longer necks. They can live over 20 years.
- Geese are a combination of **GRAY**, black and white.
- Male and female geese look **SIMILAR**, including size, shape and color.
- Geese eat **GRASS**, grains and plants.
- Geese are **MONOGAMOUS** and live permanently in pairs. This reduces courtship rituals. Geese have strong family bonds that last through many seasons and migrations. They are only territorial during the short nesting season.
- **DOMESTIC** geese can no longer fly at all. Goose down has no odor, unlike duck down.

Ducks, geese and swans are members of the same **FAMILY** of waterfowl. Like most classifications, there's often confusion. Some ducks are called geese, and some smaller geese are confused with ducks. Therefore, color and neck size are more important. Bland birds with long necks are geese while bright birds with short necks are ducks. Swans are more closely related to geese.

THEY'RE DOING THIS

LIZARDS

- Lizards are **REPTILES** (like snakes). They sun themselves to increase their body temperature.
- There are **2,500** types of lizards, including chameleons (can change color), iguanas (herbavores), geckos (the only lizards that make noise), basilisks (can walk on water), skinks (with blue tongues), Gila monsters (venomous) and Komodo dragons (largest lizard in the world).
- Lizards are found all over the **WORLD** except in the polar regions. Most live on land, either in trees or on the ground. Only a few live in the water (like the great marine iguana).
- Lizards **VARY** in size from three inches to over ten feet long.
- Lizards are covered with dry **SCALES**. They have external ear openings and clawed toes, which salamanders don't.
- Lizards have shelled eggs, which are laid on **LAND**.

When attacked, a lizard can break off its **TAIL** in order to escape. The predator is often distracted and ends up just eating the tail. Later, the lizard's tail will grow back. Some salamanders can do this as well but the new tail is gray when compared to the original tail.

IN COLD BLOOD!

SALAMANDERS

- Salamanders are **AMPHIBIANS** (like frogs). They begin their lives in water breathing with gills. As they mature, they develop lungs and breathe air. Some salamanders never get lungs and must absorb oxygen through their skin.
- There are only about **320** different types of salamanders, including newts and mudpuppies.
- Salamanders are mostly found in the **NORTHERN HEMISPHERE**. Most need to live near water and some even have webbed feet.
- Salamanders are **SMALLER**, usually four to eight inches long. The Chinese giant salamander, however, can reach almost four feet long and weigh 25 pounds.
- Salamanders have a thin, moist **SKIN** that barely prevents them from drying out.
- Salamanders produce eggs that are dependent on **WATER** or moisture.

Reptiles and amphibians are **COLD-BLOODED** (*ectothermic*). This means their bodies can't produce heat (like mammals do) and therefore they are the same temperature as the surrounding environment. When it's hot outside, they're hot; when it's cold, they're cold. If it's very cold out, they either bask in the sun, hibernate in burrows or in the mud at the bottom of a pond, migrate to warmer areas, or keep highly active. In some species, their livers produce an antifreeze. This allows their lungs and heart to stop working but they don't die. Once the weather warms up, they simply thaw out and walk away!

MAKING MOUNTAINS

GOPHERS

- Gophers are **LARGER**, about the size of a small squirrel. They also have longer tails.
- Gophers have large **TEETH**.
- Even though their eyes are very small, gophers can **SEE**. Mostly they use their whiskers and tail to feel around their tunnels when going forwards or backwards.
- Gophers are **HERBIVORES** and will eat almost any plant. They will cut the roots off beneath the surface, then pull the rest of the plant into the burrow. They'll only go above ground to grab nearby plants.
- Gophers have large cheek **POUCHES** which are used for transporting food.
- Gophers prefer **DRY** soil. They dig wider, larger and **DEEPER** tunnels.
- A gopher mound is **CRESCENT** in shape and the entrance is at an angle. Gophers always close their holes with a visible dirt plug.
- Gophers are **SOLITARY** and have their own territory.

Gophers are easily confused with other burrowing rodents. **VOLES** look like hefty mice. They don't dig their own tunnels but take over abandoned mole and gopher homes. **PRAIRIE DOGS** are larger and are frequently seen above ground.

OUT OF MOLEHILLS!

MOLES

- Moles are quite **SMALL**, usually the size of a person's thumb.
- Moles have large, front digging **CLAWS**. Their front legs are much bigger and stronger than their hind legs.
- Moles are **BLIND**. They are completely adapted to a life underground.
- Moles are **CARNIVORES**. They eat things such as grubs, earthworms, slugs, beetles, larvae and millipedes.
- Moles preserve food by coating it with a toxic **SALIVA**. They then store it in a hiding place.
- Moles prefer **MOIST** soil, which is where their food lives. They dig **SHALLOW** tunnels, often only an inch below the surface.
- Molehills are **CONICAL**, resembling a volcano. The dirt is often very chunky. They also seal up their holes but the plug doesn't show.
- Moles gather together in large **GROUPS** or families, known as *labors*.

Gophers and moles are not closely related. Gophers are rodents. Moles were classified as **INSECTIVORA** but this category is no longer used since it was mostly just meant for animals that didn't fit anywhere else. Fortunately it's been reorganized and a new group, Eulipotyphla (meaning *truly fat and blind*), is now split into:

- Hedgehogs, gymnures (or moonrats) • Moles, desmans (semi-aquatic) • Shrews • Solenodons

OYSTERS

- Oysters have a **ROUGH** shell which is irregularly **OVAL** in shape.
- Oyster shells have a **LARGER**, deeper and thicker half upon which the oyster rests.
- Oysters **ATTACH** themselves to rocks or lie on the sea bottom. They're unable to move but can be dislodged from their resting place by waves. They eat microorganisms that are carried into their shells by the current.
- The largest oyster discovered was almost 15 inches. **PEARL OYSTERS** are cultivated for quality pearls. The color is based on mineral content: white (calcium), pink (copper), purple or black (iron).

Technically a **PEARL** can be made by any clam, oyster or mussel. When a grain of sand becomes painfully stuck in the soft inner mantle, the animal coats it with a material that makes it smooth and less irritating.

WISDOM!

CLAMS

- Clams have a **SMOOTH** or slightly wavy shell. Rings indicate how old it may be. The hard-shell clam has a thick, heavy **ROUND** shell. The soft-shell clam (which has a fragile but technically not soft shell) has a thinner, more elongated shell.
- Clam shells are built with nearly **EQUAL** halves.
- Clams **MOVE** about in their environment. They open their shells and stick out a large, muscular foot that they use to push themselves along. Clams also burrow either partially or completely in the sand or mud by digging with their foot.
- **GIANT CLAMS** live in coral reefs in the Indian and Pacific oceans. They can weigh up to 500 pounds and reach five feet in length. Despite their reputation as killer clams, there are no actual cases of people being trapped and drowned by them. In reality, they can't even completely close their shells once fully grown.

Clams, mussels (small, with a longer shell), oysters and scallops (with the perfect sea shell shape) are known as **BIVALVES**, meaning they have a shell divided into two parts. They belong to the group of soft-bodied animals known as *mollusks*, which also include snails, slugs, conches, octopuses and squid.

LYNX

- Lynx are **LARGER**, weighing some 60 pounds.
- Lynx prefer the deep **FOREST** and other wooded habitats. They often live in areas with deep, winter snow.
- Lynx have a long, thick, **GRAYISH** coat with a **PLAIN** or indistinct pattern. Coat color is more reddish in the summer. They have a shaggy ruff around the face and neck.
- Lynx have **LONG** tufts of hair on their ears.
- Lynx have a shorter tail with **NO** banding. It's completely **BLACK** at the tip.
- Lynx have **LONGER** legs (especially the hind ones) and **LARGER**, wider paws, both which help in deep snow. Hair on the bottom of their paws turn their feet into snowshoes and provides traction on slippery surfaces.
- Most lynx species prefer to eat snowshoe **HARES**. The larger Eurasian lynx will often hunt deer during winter, when small prey is less abundant.
- Lynx are **SHY**, secretive animals, preferring to hide in dense forests.

There are four **SPECIES** within the Lynx genus: the Eurasian lynx (the largest, described here), the Canada lynx, the Iberian lynx (endangered) and the bobcat (smallest). While all very closely related, they still vary in size and appearance and have adapted to different habitats.

TELLING TALL TAILS!

BOBCATS

- Bobcats are **SMALLER**, at about 35 pounds. They're about twice the size of a house cat.
- Bobcats can survive in a wide **VARIETY** of habitats. They live in swamps, deserts, woodland, mountain forests and even agricultural areas.
- Bobcats have a short, **BROWNISH** coat with distinct **SPOTS**. Desert bobcats have lighter colored coats, while those in the forests have the darkest.
- Bobcats have **SHORTER** ear tufts.
- Bobcats have a slightly longer tail with **STRIPES**. The tip is black on top and **WHITE** below.
- Bobcats have **SHORTER** legs and **SMALLER** paws. They don't do as well in heavy snow, but fortunately they don't have to.
- Bobcats have an extremely **VARIED** diet and will hunt rabbits, rodents, squirrels, birds, fish and even insects.
- Bobcats are very **AGGRESSIVE**. They have a reputation of being fearless wildcats that won't back down from any fight.

The three types of lynx **LIVE** throughout Europe, Asia, and across Canada and Alaska. Bobcats only live in North America, from southern Canada down into northern Mexico.

DON'T JUMP TO

GRASSHOPPERS

- Grasshoppers are **LARGER**, ranging from one to five inches. Their antennae are **SHORT** (about half of their body length) and horn-shaped.
- Grasshoppers are **HERBIVORES**, feeding on plants and crops.
- Grasshoppers chirp (called *stridulation*) by rubbing their long, spiky hind **LEGS** against their hard, front wings. Both males and females can do this but the males are much, much louder. Each species has its own chirp.
- Grasshoppers hear through an auditory organ (*tympanum*) on the base of their **ABDOMENS**.
- Grasshoppers are active during the **DAY**.
- Female grasshoppers lay their eggs in **GROUPS** (about 20 eggs) below the soil surface.

Grasshoppers, locusts, crickets and katydids all share a common ancestor. **CICADAS** are in a completely different group of winged insects more closely related to aphids. **LOCUSTS** are a species of short-horned grasshoppers. Normally they're shy and solitary, but sometimes a food shortage can trigger a chemical change in the new nymphs (or young), turning them into migrating adults. Huge swarms of millions (even billions) of insects can blot out the sun and strip a field in a matter of hours.

CONCLUSIONS!

CRICKETS

- Crickets are **SMALLER**, rarely measuring over two inches long. True crickets have **LONG** antennae and somewhat flattened bodies. Their forewings are also shorter.
- Crickets are herbivores and **SCAVENGERS**. They will eat almost anything but prefer seeds, rotting leaves, fruit and dead insects. They will hunt smaller, weaker crickets if food is scarce.
- Only male crickets chirp. They make their noise by rubbing together special parts of their front **WINGS**. A cricket can produce four different types of calls. The wings also act as amplifiers, which is how such a small creature can make so much noise.
- Crickets detect sound by auditory organs on their **FORELEGS**.
- Crickets are **CREPUSCULAR**, only venturing out during the twilight hours.
- Female crickets lay their eggs **SINGLY** in the earth or in plant stems. They have a long needle-like egg-laying organ called an *ovipositor*.

STRIDULATION is a means of communication in order to warn other insects of danger, mark a territory or attract a mate. It is temperature dependent, with warmer weather resulting in a higher number of chirps per minute. Unfortunately there are many variables (the type of cricket, its age, whether it's hungry, if there are other males nearby and so on), so crickets aren't very accurate thermometers. The biggest disadvantage is that it lets predators know exactly where they are!

CAN THEY WEASEL

WEASELS

- Weasels belong to the **DOG-LIKE** carnivores (Caniformia), including dogs, bears, walruses, seals, skunks and raccoons.
- Weasels live on **MANY** continents including Africa, Europe, Asia and the America. Some (such as otters) are aquatic, living in rivers and oceans.
- Most weasels are **SOLITARY** and **NOCTURNAL**, although depending on the climate and season, they'll also hunt during the day.
- Weasels have a very high **METABOLISM** and need to eat up to 40% of their body weight daily.
- Some weasel **SPECIES** are:
  - The *least weasel* (at about two ounces) is the smallest carnivore in the world. It can take down much larger prey with a quick, fatal bite to the neck.
  - The *ferret* is the domesticated form of the European *polecat*.
  - The *stoat* or short-tailed weasel has a black-tipped tail. It's often called an *ermine* when wearing its pure white winter coat.
  - The *mink* is semiaquatic and often raised for its fur.

The weasel family is the largest and most diverse of carnivorous mammals. There are **EIGHT** subfamilies:

- Weasels, most polecats, ferrets, minks, stoats/ermines
- Otters
- African polecats, zorillas, grisons
- Ferret-badgers
- Martens, sables, wolverines, fishers
- European and Asian badgers
- Honey badgers (in Africa)
- American badgers

OUT OF THIS ONE?

MONGOOSES

- Mongooses belong to the **CAT-LIKE** carnivores (Feliformia), which also includes all cats, civets, hyenas and aardwolves. Mongooses have narrow, horizontal pupils (like deer).
- Mongooses mostly live in **AFRICA** but some are in Madagascar and southern Eurasia.
- Most mongooses are **SOCIAL** and **DIURNAL**. Many live in groups ranging from six up to 50 individuals. Each member has a specific job. Some hunt while others stay home to take care of the young, sick and old.
- Many mongooses have the ability to kill venomous **SNAKES**. Along with extreme speed and agility, they're largely immune to snake and scorpion venom, although repeated strikes could sicken or kill them. Because of this, they were often kept as pets.
- **SPECIES** of mongoose include:
  - The *kusimanse* or dwarf mongoose lives in the swamps and forests of Africa.
  - The *banded mongoose* has rough fur with several dark bars across its back.
  - The *yellow mongoose* bases its colony around an alpha breeding pair and their offspring.
  - *Meerkats* are well-known for standing upright to watch for predators.

The mongoose family is relatively small. There are **TWO** subfamlies:

- Indian mongooses, Egyptian mongooses, slender mongooses
- Dwarf mongooses, yellow mongooses, banded mongooses, meerkats (or suricates)

THEY'LL TURN YOUR

TWO-TOED SLOTHS

- Two-toed sloths have **TWO** toes on their front feet and three on their back feet. Technically they should be called two-*fingered* sloths! There are **TWO** species.
- Two-toed sloths are **LARGER**. They can get over two feet long and weigh up to 17 pounds. Their arms are the **SAME** length as their legs.
- Two-toed sloths **LACK** a tail and have **46 RIBS**. In order to breathe easily while hanging upside down, its internal organs are anchored to its rib cage and hip bones.
- Two-toed sloths have **SIX** neck bones. Most mammals have seven. A two-toed sloth can only turn its head **90 DEGREES**.
- Two-toed sloths are **NOCTURNAL**. They also move **FASTER** (which still isn't very fast).
- Two-toed sloths are more **DEFENSIVE**.
- Female two-toed sloths outnumber the males **ELEVEN** to one! The males lead solitary lives while the females live in small groups.

Two- and three-toed sloths are not close **RELATIVES**. They belong to the group Xenartha (meaning *strange joints*) which also includes armadillos, anteaters and the extinct giant ground sloths. Little is known about their common ancestor other than it lived on the ground over 40 million years ago and was the size of a bear. Through convergent evolution, sloths ended up looking the same on the outside but very different on the inside. They can not mate with each other.

WORLD UPSIDE DOWN!
THREE-TOED SLOTHS

- Three-toed sloths have **THREE** toes on their front and back feet. There are **FOUR** species, including the pygmy sloth.
- Three-toed sloths are **SMALLER**, with a length of 18 inches and a weight of ten pounds. Their arms are **LONGER** than their legs.
- Three-toed sloths have a short **TAIL** and **28 RIBS** (humans have 24).
- Three-toed sloths have **NINE** neck bones. The more neck bones one has, the more the neck can rotate. Three-toed sloths can therefore turn their heads **270 DEGREES**.
- Three-toed sloths are mostly **DIURNAL**, although they can be active at night as well. They are **SLOWER**, sometimes not moving at all an entire day. They are better swimmers.
- Three-toed sloths are more **DOCILE**. These are the ones people have as pets.
- Three-toed sloths have an **EQUAL** number of males and females.

The word **SLOTH** means *laziness*. But sloths aren't lazy, they're efficient. Because they eat a low-energy diet of leaves, they live in "energy-saving" mode. Hanging is far easier than balancing, allowing sloths to have one-fourth the muscle mass of similar-sized animals. Movement attracts predators, so hiding still under branches keeps them safe. Their slow lifestyle allows algae to grow in their fur, camouflaging them even more. They have to live in warmer climates because their metabolism is so slow that they're unable to shiver.

DON'T CRANE YOUR

CRANES

- The crane family has been around for 40 million years. Cranes are closely related to **COOTS**, rails and moorhens.
- The **WHOOPING CRANE** (shown here) has a wing span of almost seven feet. Other species are the sandhill crane, Siberian crane and African crowned cranes.
- Cranes have **SMALLER** heads, which enables them to fly with their necks **STRETCHED** out, like a goose.
- Cranes have steady, **QUICK** wing movements during flight.
- Cranes are very **SOCIAL** and gather in large groups in wide open spaces, away from trees. They also fly in formation, similar to geese.
- Cranes are **OMNIVORES** and can adapt to any type of food, depending on availability and season. In aquatic areas they eat shrimp, frogs, fish, snails and insects, while in fields they eat berries, acorns and seeds. They'll even eat small reptiles, mammals and birds.

While many **WATER BIRDS** look very similar, they're not necessarily closely related to each other. This mostly has to do with skeletal and other internal differences. Swans and geese are closer to chickens and turkeys; cranes are closer to sandpipers and puffins; and herons and storks are closer to penguins and albatrosses.

NECK TOO FAR!

HERONS

- Herons are related to egrets, bitterns and **PELICANS**.
- The **GREAT BLUE HERON** (pictured below) has a wing span of up to six feet. Other popular species include the little blue heron, green heron and black-crowned night heron.
- Herons have **HEAVIER** heads, beaks and necks. When it flies, a heron must pull its head in, thereby giving its neck an **S-SHAPE**.
- Herons have **SLOW** wing beats.
- Herons are usually **SOLITARY**, hunting and flying alone. They've even been known to attack other herons. They perch and nest in trees.
- Herons are **CARNIVOROUS**. They mostly eat fish but will also catch salamanders, turtles, snakes, rodents and birds. They often stand very still in shallow water, waiting for an unwary fish to swim by, then strike quickly with a rapid thrust of the bill.

STORKS are also large, long-legged, long-necked wading birds that look a lot like herons and cranes but belong to a completely different order. They are famous for building large platform nests in trees, on rock ledges and even on rooftops.

FLYING SQUIRRELS

- Flying squirrels are **PLACENTAL** mammals in the rodent family.
- Flying squirrels are mostly found in **ASIA**, but there are species in the Americas and Europe.
- Flying squirrels are larger. Some species weigh up to five **POUNDS**.
- Flying squirrel babies are **LARGER**. Two to seven babies are born in a **NEST**. They're helpless, blind and naked. After one month, they open their eyes and have fur. At two months old, they learn to glide.
- Flying squirrels are similar to **SQUIRRELS** but with a few adaptations. Their limbs are longer but their hands and feet are shorter. They still have the nice fluffy tail.
- Flying squirrels have a **SHORTER** lifespan of only about six years.
- Flying squirrels are **OMNIVORES**. They eat berries, nuts, seeds, insects, fungi, spiders, bird eggs and more.

Flying squirrels and sugar gliders are completely **UNRELATED** but are the result of convergent evolution. Gliding is an efficient way to get to food and evade predators. Different types of gliders include flying squirrels, anomalures (scaly-tailed flying squirrels and flying mice), colugos (flying lemurs), the feather-tailed glider (the smallest mammalian glider), the greater glider, and flying phalangers (gliding possums, including sugar gliders).

YOUR HEAD?

SUGAR GLIDERS

- Sugar gliders are **MARSUPIAL** mammals.
- Sugar gliders live in **AUSTRALIA**, Tasmania, New Guinea and some surrounding islands.
- Sugar gliders are smaller, only four to five **OUNCES**.
- Sugar glider babies are **SMALLER** than a peanut. Only one or two babies are born. They crawl into their mother's **POUCH** and continue to grow for the next two months. About two months later, they're ready to set out on their own.
- Sugar gliders are similar to **POSSUMS**. They have a fuzzy, thin, partially prehensile tail as well as an opposable toe on each foot.
- Sugar gliders live **LONGER**, up to 15 years.
- In summer, sugar gliders are primarily **INSECTIVORES**, but will eat most anything. In winter they're mostly **EXUDATIVORES**, feeding on sugary tree sap, gum and resin. They also consume sweet plant nectar and pollen.

Flying squirrels and sugar gliders don't **FLY** like birds or bats do. Instead, a thin piece of furry skin stretched between their arms and legs (called a *patagium*) acts like a parachute, allowing them to extend their leaps between trees. They control their glide with their limbs and tail.

LLAMAS

- Llamas are **LARGER**. They weigh 250 to 450 pounds and can reach a height of six feet.
- Llamas have a **LONGER** face with less hair on their heads. They have **CURVED**, banana-shaped ears.
- Llamas live at **LOWER** elevations, below 8,000 feet.
- Llamas were bred as **PACK** animals to carry heavy loads for long distances. Alpacas, on the other hand, could not even carry a small child.
- Llamas are independent, confident and **BRAVE**. They're highly protective and serve as good guards for alpacas, sheep and other small livestock. They're also known for spitting when they feel threatened.

Llamas and alpacas live in the Andean highlands in South America. They were domesticated by the Incas some 6,000 years ago. Llamas **DESCEND** from wild guanacos, and alpacas from wild vicuñas.

SPITTING IMAGE!

ALPACAS

- Alpacas are **SMALLER**, weighing from 100 to 180 pounds. They are about five feet tall.
- Alpaca faces are more **BLUNT**. They often have a large tuft of hair on their heads that falls into their eyes. They have **STRAIGHT**, spear-shaped ears.
- Alpacas live at **HIGHER** elevations of 12,000 feet.
- Alpacas were bred for their **WOOL**. Each soft, silky coat produces about 13 pounds of fiber. A llama, with its course outer guard hairs over a short undercoat, only produces about four pounds of fiber, even though it's almost twice the size.
- Alpacas are very gentle, quiet and **SHY**. They prefer to live in herds. They rarely bite, spit or kick.

Llamas and alpacas can **BREED** and produce a fertile offspring, but it would have neither the strength nor the lovely fleece of its parents.

ABOUT THE AUTHOR

F. Elza Cooperman resides in Boulder, Colorado, USA. She has spent her life traveling and exploring, which has led to her appreciation and curiosity about the wide diversity that this beautiful planet has to offer. She hopes this book will encourage others to enjoy it as well.

ABOUT THE ILLUSTRATOR

Aleksandar Andjelkovic lives in Niš, Serbia. He's a professional illustrator and graphic designer. His passion since childhood has been comics and 2D animation and he currently works in the game industry. He loves animals and is very glad to have been able to illustrate this book.

10123059R00062

Made in the USA
San Bernardino, CA
27 November 2018